MW01253869

Love and Human Remains

Love and Human Remains

Brad Fraser

Playwrights Canada Press
Toronto • Canada

Playwrights Canada Press
The Canadian Drama Publisher
215 Spadina Ave., Suite 230, Toronto, Ontario, Canada M5T 2C7
phone 416.703.0013 fax 416.408.3402
orders@playwrightscanada.com • www.playwrightscanada.com

The publisher acknowledges the support of the Canadian taxpayers through the Government of Canada Book Publishing Industry Development Program, the Canada Council for the Arts, the Ontario Arts Council, and the Ontario Media Development Corporation.

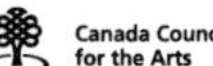

Front cover image: Francis Bacon, *Figure in Movement*, 1978 © Francis Bacon Estate/DACS, London, 2006/Licensed by SODART Montreal.
Cover design: JLArt and Brad Fraser
Production Editor: Michael Petrasek

Library and Archives Canada Cataloguing in Publication

Fraser, Brad, 1959-
Love and human remains / Brad Fraser.

Originally written as Unidentified human remains and the true nature of love.
ISBN 0-88754-914-4

I. Title.

PS8561.R294L68 2006 C812'.54 C2006-905611-0

First Playwrights Canada Press edition: November 2006
Second printing: August 2008
Printed and bound by Printco at Scarborough, Canada

For Jeffrey, B.J., Ken, Carol, Kate and Kimm.

Introduction

Writing the Play

I was fucked up. Totally.

Spring, 1984. *Wolfboy*, my most successful play to that point, starring a very young Keanu Reeves, had bombed in an ill-steered production in Toronto. Concurrently, I'd discovered the man of my dreams was a psychopathic liar and I'd lost my job at a Malaysian restaurant. I borrowed a hundred dollars from a friend and, leaving everything with the psycho lover and a resentful roommate, caught the first Greyhound back to Edmonton—a particularly charming way to view much of this great country.

My career in the theatre was over. As far as I was concerned the stage was a dead medium. The only people who seemed to be interested in it were the grant-happy ex-hippies who ran it and the geriatrics who seemed to support it out of nothing more than a sense of obligation coupled with old-world pretension. I was bitter.

In Edmonton I got re-involved with a number of old friends and found a job waiting tables at one of the city's better restaurants. I partied a lot. I bad-mouthed Toronto.

I stopped mentioning the theatre. I wrote a novel. I drew page after page of comic book stories that were never completed. I toyed with the idea of going to university to study medicine. I discovered the early Edmonton Fringe Festival, which Chinook Theatre director Brian Paisley had started a few years earlier. With the help of Workshop West Theatre I wrote, directed and produced another play.

The play was *Chainsaw Love*, a script I'd started to develop in the very first incarnation of the Tarragon Theatre Playwright's Circle. After that initial stab at the play I'd dropped it, feeling that the Tarragon experience had seemed to be more about the artistic director trying to help me write a certain kind of play—the Tarragon kind of play with one set and four characters and lots of talking and internal revelations about events that happen off-stage—rather than aiding me in finding the best way to write the play I was trying to write (which involved none of those things). However, the experience also allowed me to meet and interact with such wonderfully imaginative people as Steve Petch, Atom Egoyan and Robin Fulford, to name just a few, and that made it more than worthwhile.

Despite some major shortcomings in *Chainsaw Love*, which took itself far too seriously and could have been half as long, the show became a bit of an Edmonton Fringe legend. I'm sure the hammer-in-the-head and meat-hook-in-the-back scenes, as well as actress Kate Newby's outstanding performance as the mentally challenged daughter, had something to do with this. Almost everyone in the first two rows of the house was guaranteed to be splattered with blood by at least one of the show's many stabbings, beatings or eviscerations. We were a popular, if not critical, quasi-hit.

But I knew something was missing. The Grand-Guignol horror of *Chainsaw Love* was interesting, but it still didn't do what I hoped to do theatrically. It was too easy for the audience to disengage emotionally from the over-the-top antics of the child-molesting cannibal family that inhabits the script. I wanted to make people laugh but I didn't want to let them off the hook. The wackiness of *Chainsaw Love* definitely let them off the hook.

What I liked most about that first Fringe experience was the audience that attended so enthusiastically. This audience seemed to be half as old and not nearly as rich as your average theatre-goer. This audience had the potential to develop and grow rather than age and die. I found great hope in this. Enough hope to return tentatively to the theatre again.

That summer I became part of a play development group sponsored by Workshop West Theatre, then run by artistic director and founder Gerry Potter. Gerry created a workshop situation that allowed me and a number of other actors and writers to play with and explore ideas in a forum that focused on process rather than hard results.

Frustrated with the comic-book world I'd used as my inspiration so far, I decided to look at much more reality-based ideas. At twenty-seven I could feel my adult self separating from my younger self and I wanted to examine that phenomenon and the concerns it carried. A number of exercises were done with the actors, some based on performer-generated scenarios and others based on thumbnail sketches I'd write quickly and bring into rehearsal. The process was perhaps slightly over-earnest, but something began to emerge from it. I started to write scenes between characters who had been long-time friends, all of them desperate for some love in their lives and some hope in their world.

But something was missing. Some crucial story element that would elevate the piece from being the usual bit of CBCish drama to something more entertaining, something more timely.

That's when they found the body.

The body belonged to a hairdresser who went missing after an evening of partying at a local discotheque. She had been sexually assaulted, tortured, murdered and mutilated. Certain details of the crime were so horrific they were withheld from the public so they could be used to implicate the killer, who was eventually caught.

While the horror of the crime was arresting enough, there was actually another reason the event jarred me so much. The body had been found beneath the bridge at the Genesee power plant outside Edmonton.

I had canoed underneath that very bridge within the last four weeks. It'd been on a weekend camping trip with my best friend of many years.

That got me to thinking.

And I thought, "What if it was my best friend who killed this woman?"

Please keep in mind that this was 1986, years before the serial killer became the hoary chestnut of dramatic devices that it has since become.

From that one question all kinds of ideas, images and memories started to fly together. It was one of those all-too-rare moments I have as a writer when one simple idea suddenly breeds myriad dramatic possibilities. And even though a lot of these possibilities were informed by my vast repertoire of comic book/television/pop-cult devices, many of these possibilities were also informed by my own life and the lives of the people I knew.

For the first time I decided to record and interpret the things that happened to me and around me. I wanted to distill the world I was living in down to its most basic elements and, hopefully, understand it.

So I started to write.

But before I actually put anything on paper, I got a felt pen and a small piece of bristol board and wrote my favorite Sex Pistols slogan on it. "No rules." That, I decided, would be the only parameter for what I was about to attempt.

All the rules I'd been taught about writing for the theatre went out the window.

Keep the number of characters small to make it cheaper to produce. I used seven.

Limit the number of sets to keep production costs down and to avoid confusing the audience. I set scenes wherever they needed to be set. In bars, bedrooms, cars, rooftops, whatever. The designers and the audience would have to use their imaginations.

Develop long, well-constructed scenes through the use of mostly expository dialogue. I wanted scenes that pulsed and flowed into one another with no regard to naturalistic space or linear time. I wanted my characters always to operate in the here and now and to refer to the past even less than we do in real life.

Sex and violence never work in the theatre. I hoped I could find a way to theatricalize sex and violence that would be illuminative rather than exploitive.

As I wrote this first draft I was doing something I hadn't actually done since I wrote the very first draft of *Mutants*, the first show I had produced. I was writing a show I'd like to go and see. I wasn't worried about who would produce it or direct it. I was simply writing it for myself. And I was having a hell of a good time doing it.

The serial killer plotline gave me a framework for all of my mid-1980s preoccupations. I used actual events from my life as springboards to create comic and dramatic situations that went much further and with more clarity than real life ever does.

Characters who started out as sketches of people I knew began taking on lives and characteristics of their own. They evolved. They mutated. They grew. By the time the show reached the first draft stage each of the characters had demanded and achieved a free life, independent of their non-fiction template.

There were nights when I couldn't wait to complete my waiter shift so I could get home to see where the play would go next. I had the most basic storyline in my head, but when I sat down at my little blue plastic Smith Corona portable typewriter nightly for two or three intense hours with Candy, David, Benita, et al., I was watching an adventure take place on a stage in my mind. The entire process was a strange combination of my perverse pleasure in breaking the rules and a sort of automatic writing that spilled from my subconscious onto the page.

It was during the writing of this show that I started smoking pot while I was writing. It seemed to make it easier not to say no and censor myself before I'd even tried something. Pot was invaluable in helping me find the shattered structure of the piece. Peter Gabriel's album *So* rarely left the turntable while I was writing. Certain songs, "Red Rain," "In Your Eyes," "Mercy Street," were played again and again. Occasionally Peter was relieved by Kate Bush (*Hounds of Love*), Lou Reed (*Transformer*) or, when I had to evoke some David and Bernie atmosphere, any Bruce Springsteen album would do.

When I was stuck for a structural idea, I didn't think back to other plays I'd seen or read, instead I switched on MuchMusic and glutted myself on rock videos, dove into a reread of Alan Moore's amazing run on DC Comic's *Swamp Thing*, ran to the movie theatre to catch something like Paul Verhoven's *The Fourth Man*, or flew off to Flashback, Edmonton's best dance bar, to bop to tunes by Berlin, Vicious Pink, Michael Bow, etc.

I made a conscious effort to take the language I knew, the language of the people I knew, into the theatre in the hope that doing so might draw them to see a play.

Early in the writing of the play I made another sign to hang on the wall before my typewriter. This second, longer, sign read: "This is not a play about a serial killer. This is a play about a guy who finds out his best friend is a serial killer."

Everything I'd spent the last eight years doing or thinking about fed the play. My unhappy years in Toronto, my struggle to accept my sexuality, my relationships with men and women, the horrifying spectre of AIDS and the future havoc it would wreak in the lives of all of us—everything poured out of me into this story of seven lonely young people searching for love, and it all made a sort of dramatic sense.

Then, after months of working on the script, after writing the harrowing climactic scene between David and Bernie that ends with the gunshot and the siren, I laid my head on the keyboard of my typewriter and cried.

I cried for a long time. And when I stopped crying I felt very clean and very light. And I read the entire play again, from beginning to end, and realized that not only did the show still lack an ending, but it also needed a title.

The ending was fairly painless. I simply resolved the play with a scene that allowed some kind of emotional release without becoming too sentimental. I hoped Candy's pizza business and Kane's emotional ineptitude would cut through David's pain. I tried to construct an ending that allowed all the script's earlier horror and darkness to be acknowledged while still presenting some minor glimmer of hope to those leaving the theatre.

Not everyone thinks I was entirely successful. From the beginning there was a very vocal contingent who suggested that David's journey would never be complete if it wasn't he that said the words "I love you" at the end of the play. I was quite satisfied with leaving the audience knowing that David is ready to say "I love you" but isn't allowed to by Candy and Kane. Benita's taking of the line for David made emotional, if not technical, sense to me.

Then there was another group that felt the entire final scene could be cut and was just a cop-out anyway. Whatever. All I knew was that I needed some light at the end of the play, some sense of hope. The ending worked for me.

Truly wonderful titles for plays are like really great sexual partners. They always present themselves at unusual times and are never what you expect them to be. Also, they're worth their weight in gold. A number of ideas were floating around my head at the time including, *Dead Boys Dancing*, *Casual Slaughter*, and *Fresh Meat*. Catchy, but they all read a little punk rock retro and I wanted something that felt more late 1980s.

Some years earlier, at the height of my earlier twenties morbidness, the same time when friends and I considered it fun to get high on acid and go to graveyards and read tombstones at three a.m., I'd pulled a small police poster from a gay bar bulletin board.

The poster was headed by two strange photographs of a forensically reconstructed face. Each photo showed the smooth, unearthly face from a slightly different angle. Beneath the photo was the headline "unidentified human remains." Beneath the headline was a description of the nameless cadaver that had been found in a septic tank at a farmhouse near a small town outside Edmonton. The man, whom they speculated to be between five feet six inches and six one—that's how decomposed he was—had been sexually assaulted, tortured and mutilated before he was killed.

I kept this poster, not only for its graphic shock appeal, but also because the idea of someone being so invisible that his body couldn't be identified fascinated me. Here was the perfect title for my play. Unidentified human remains. This was the imagery. Mutilated people missed by no one, friends or family. Those were my characters.

But the title still felt incomplete to me. It only spoke of a portion of the play. Something was missing. Something that told people that the show wasn't just about the horrors of the world, but that it had another side. A funny, playful, poignant side. A human side. A side about people searching for love. Not just one kind of love, all kinds of love, any kind of love. The true nature of love. And there it was. Too long. Unwieldy. Certain to be shortened in unfortunate ways in the future and correctly remembered by nearly no one. But it was the title. *Unidentified Human Remains and the True Nature of Love*. It made me laugh. It felt right. Everyone told me it would never work. I knew then I had the perfect title.

So I started sending it out to theatres across the country. I knew the play was good. I was sure I'd have no problem finding an interested producer.

Getting the Play Produced

I was wrong. Nobody wanted to produce it.

Workshop West gave me a reading and workshop of the epic first draft of the show. The play was too long and overstated at that time, but everyone acknowledged that there was a workable, even good play to be carved out of that first draft. The humour and the suspense both worked very well. However, while he was eager to see another draft, Gerry Potter had no interest in making a production commitment.

An early draft sent to Urjo Kareda at the Tarragon resulted in a letter praising the characters and the unorthodox structure but condemning the entire serial killer framework as sensationalist and unworkable. I knew what he meant, but I wasn't looking for someone to help me narrow my vision. I wanted to expand it.

Clarke Rogers at Theatre Passe Muraille was enthusiastic. I was wary, still smarting from the *Wolfboy* experience. However, everyone was impressed about a new director/dramaturge named Peter Hinton who seemed right for the show, so I wasn't totally standoffish. Unfortunately, Clarke was ousted from the theatre, and despite some strong support for the show by Peter Hinton and then-dramaturge Deborah Porter, the play was dropped.

I decided to take another run at the script, hoping another rewrite would make the play so strong someone would have to produce it.

I read through all the responses to the play, looked for points that were valid or repeated, and set to work on a new draft.

I worked hard to make the play as clean and dynamic as possible. Making sentences shorter. Making my intentions clearer. Listening for patterns of speech in everyday language that I could theatricalize. Finding different ways to vary the rhythm and flow of the play through dialogue and action. Sharpening up scenes. Replacing images that didn't quite make it with more vivid ones. Making the dramatic moments truly dramatic and humorous moments truly humorous.

I may have broken all the rules while writing the play, but I had to follow one of the oldest rules of dramatics in the rewrite.

That is, eliminate anything that doesn't directly relate to action, character or atmosphere. This edited over an hour from the script and gave it a stronger focus and more impact.

I sent the revised play everywhere I could think of, hungry for a reaction and a production. I really felt I'd gotten it right. That I had an exciting script on my hands. Something that felt like a hit. They had to see that now. But they didn't.

Reactions were more enthusiastic, but always tempered with concerns that the piece really was too dark, bleak and angry to appeal to a general audience. There was a lot of praise for the writing, but no offers to produce.

At this point in my life I was feeling trapped and stale in Edmonton. I was spending far too much time working in restaurants and hanging out in gay bars. Hungry for a change, I moved to Calgary with a couple of friends where, within minutes of arriving, I was spending far too much time working in restaurants and hanging out in gay bars.

I'd known Allan MacInnis, who was an artistic associate at Alberta Theatre Projects at that time, for a number of years. He'd been supportive about an earlier draft and it was through his arrangement and the fact that *Unidentified Human Remains and the True Nature of Love* had won the Alberta Culture Playwrighting Competition that year, that the play received a staged reading during the 1988 playRites Festival.

Prior to the public reading of the play, reaction from the theatre staff was subdued to say the least. I heard through the grapevine that certain parties found the show offensive. Others had dismissed it as unworkable. The actors, during the few hours of round-table rehearsal the public readings were given, seemed uncertain about what they were doing. No one had a clue what to make of the show. And worse, Calgary was in the throes of the 1988 Olympics. What if the play somehow tarnished a foreign opinion of ATP? After all, the world's eyes were on every element of Calgary, cultural as well as athletic.

The audience that showed up for the two readings had no such reservations. From the moment the actors started to read I knew I had them. As soon as the audience started to react audibly, mostly with laughter, the actors realized that the show they were doing had a great deal of humour in it and loosened up. Even though it was still too long and act two needed some strengthening, the audience was listening—and liking it.

I heard it. Allan MacInnis heard it. Bob White, who was taking over Allan's position at that time, heard it. And, most importantly, D. Michael Dobbin, artistic director at Alberta Theatre Projects, heard it.

A short time later I was offered a playwright residency at the theatre for the following season. Although Bob White was very direct about championing the play for the playRites Festival of the following year, everyone else was less eager to jump on the bandwagon. The festival was ATP's platform to explore and take risks, but the exploration and risks involved in producing *Remains* were deemed possibly suicidal by the powers that be.

Both Bob and I spent the next three months praising the play and pushing it on Dobbin and the other playRites decision-makers every chance we could. It had been over three years since I had started writing it and I was beginning to feel it would never be produced.

Finally, after much hemming and hawing, the play was announced for the festival. Both Bob and I were jubilant. Everyone else was nervous.

The Production

As has always been the case with any of the five festivals I've taken part in, all the really important decisions (casting, designers, promotion, etc.) had to take a back seat to the regular ATP season of contemporary middle-of-the-road plays. This despite the fact that playRites is the only thing that distinguishes this mid-size Calgary theatre from any of its many counterparts throughout North America.

But because of this back-benching of the festival until the season was sorted out, all of the writers had to wait until the last moment to find out who would be in the acting company, who the designers of the shows would be and, most importantly, who would direct.

Initially, I had assumed Allan MacInnis would direct the play, but he was off to another engagement at the other end of the country. So the search for another director began.

The few people I felt I might be able to work with, Roy Surette, Duncan McIntosh, Joanna McIntyre, were already booked for the busy January/February part of the theatre season or uninterested. I ventured forth Peter Hinton's name. By this time Peter and I had had a number of in-depth discussions about the play and I liked his bizarre energy and his belief in the script. This suggestion was rejected by Dobbin. I suspect he felt, with a play that was already considered controversial, a director unknown to him would be a wild card he'd rather not play.

So, with one of those decisions that one comes to examine and question throughout one's life, I decided not to fight for Peter and to give in to Michael on his suggestion of Susan Ferley for director of *Unidentified Human Remains and the True Nature of Love*. Both Michael and I thought that Susan, whose smart, frothy production of Sky Gilbert's *The Postman Only Rings Twice* had impressed me a few years earlier, would bring a sensitivity and awareness to the material, hopefully, to illuminate the play on a brand new level.

What we had really done was set in gear events and personalities that would create a scenario combining the best parts of *Children of the Damned, The Crucible* and *Who's Afraid of Virginia Woolf?* in a Mixmaster stuffed with the hearts and other vital organs of most everyone who took part in that year's festivities.

It started with the warnings. The theatre began issuing them from the second the play's production was announced. Every mention of the show gave a warning: Warning. Foul language. Warning. Nudity. Warning. Controversial lifestyle. Warning. May offend. Warning. May ruin our festival and our theatre. Warning. May not work.

The original cast of *Unidentified Human Remains and the True Nature of Love* was a particularly piquant mix of personalities, numbering among them my then-lover, an ex-lover, and a former roommate, all of whom were so close in personality to the characters they were playing it should have been illegal to do so.

The director and I had decided, early in the proceedings, that I would keep a careful eye on what was going on but maintain a distant presence. I hoped to provide some kind of objective view of the proceedings. Susan felt my playing that role would be helpful to her process as well. Keeping me distant enough not to be looking over her shoulder but ensuring I was there if she needed me.

The first reading went well. The entire company showed up and laughed a lot. The actors, buoyed by the reaction, had a terrific time reading their parts. I glanced over at the director on the far end of the table and watched her listening and nodding her head. She wasn't laughing.

The next day the *Remains* company was moved into a dusty concrete basement and rehearsals began.

The director liked to spend a lot of time around the table discussing the show and "verbing." Verbing is finding an action word for every line in the play in order to keep the play active. It's also a very good actor exercise, pushing the performers to be very specific in their approach to the text from the outset. It's also a laborious, often boring process and I could sense some animosity building in certain actors. I'd drop in for ten minutes here and there and then move onto whichever one of my many playwright-in-residence duties I had to attend to. Each time I dropped into rehearsal the energy in the room seemed to have decreased more and more.

My then-lover would come home from rehearsal clearly pissed off. We had a let's-not-discuss-work-at-home rule that was usually never followed. Although the then-lover would attempt to be diplomatic about the situation, it emerged that some of the cast was getting concerned because the director still had them all sitting around the table in the second week of a weirdly constructed repertory rehearsal schedule and they were antsy to get on their feet and get the play moving.

I dropped by rehearsal the next day, as it happened, the day the director started moving towards getting the play up on its feet. The actors seemed relieved and clamped onto the activity immediately. But as she went back to refine her work more and more, or to discuss the reason for a particular moment's importance, I saw the actors' energy flag.

Everyone seemed frustrated and angry. They were banished to a basement and forced to rehearse some weird play they had no context for. It felt like everyone was avoiding taking control of the experience because everyone wanted to evade whatever blame might result after opening. All the actors knew nudity would be required for the show and were completely prepared to shed their clothes at the appropriate time. (The only exception to this rule was an actor who had refused the nudity rider because "it would upset his wife.") But the overly sensitive treatment the nudity was getting from the director was starting to make the actors self-conscious. In fact, everything about the experience was so nurturing and sensitive that the actors didn't have a clue what they were doing. The only message they seemed to be getting was that they were performing in what must be one of the most horrible plays ever. Why else would everyone keep apologizing about it so much?

I started showing up at rehearsal more often, making it clear to the director that I was there if she needed me. Actors started calling me at home after rehearsal just to chat. Others cornered me for lunch or on staircases or walked with me to rehearsal, each of them desperate for some clue as to how to make this play work. I discussed things in general terms, pointed out portions of text that might help them. The actors started calling more and more often. Since I was not the director, I became uncomfortable. I felt I was doing her job and I hadn't been hired to do so.

The following night the then-lover came home from rehearsal and let everything out. They were all fed up. None of them knew what they were doing. No one liked the play. No one liked the process. They still hadn't blocked most of the play and they were opening in a week.

The telephone rang. It was another one of the actors. Someone else called. It was the same story. The skipper wasn't skipping. The ship was adrift. The crew was in a panic.

I wanted to scream. I wanted to cry. I was trying desperately to stay away. To be objective. To stay positive. To not alienate people. But I knew I had to address this situation the next day.

I walked in shortly after rehearsal had started. The cast was sitting in the stage area sullenly staring at their scripts. The director sat in a chair before them, her script open on a music stand before her. She was writing in her script in pencil and questioning someone's use of a specific verb.

I interrupted and laid my cards on the table. By this point I'd been approached by almost everyone in the show and many of them seemed to have a particular problem with the directorial process. They all felt insecure with what they were doing with the play and I thought perhaps it was time we all discussed this face-to-face, rather than over the phone or in the bar after rehearsal.

The director looked at me. She didn't know what I was talking about. There was no problem with her process. She didn't sense anything "negative" about the rehearsal process so far.

I suggested maybe she was too preoccupied with whatever it was she was doing with the play to notice. All the actors but two had expressed powerful reservations about her work with the play and we had to talk about it and get this production back on the rails.

I turned to the actors expectantly. They'd back me up.

Not one of them was looking at me.

I raised my eyebrows expectantly.

Someone murmured something about "no real problems."

I couldn't believe it. Not one of them would repeat any of the things they said to me.

Fine. I was in so far it would hurt both of us to pull out now. I went for it. I repeated what had been said to me. I voiced the actors' concerns for them, as I now saw they expected me to. Once I opened up, most of the actors voiced some of their frustrations, albeit in a much more diplomatic manner than I'd ever heard them use. The director's reaction was hard to gauge. She wasn't sure what to do. I asked the actors what they needed to get on with doing their jobs. The answer was unanimous. Blocking. They needed to know what world this play lived in. What rhythms it had. How it moved.

The director, overwhelmed, retreated to the back of the rehearsal hall. I asked her if she minded if I ran the actors through a quick physical exercise to give them some of what they seemed to be asking for. She didn't say yes, but she didn't say no, so I went ahead with it anyway.

I proceeded to block the entire opening of the show with the stylized staccato movement I knew it needed. We got through the very difficult sequence leading into the first scene between David and Candy and it seemed the actors suddenly got it. They were all quite secure with the actual scenes as Susan had taken them through them, but the poetic, connecting underscore of the play, both vocal and physical, hadn't been addressed and it wasn't some directorial gimmick to be imposed on the play later. It was an integral part of the structure of the storytelling.

This seemed to placate everyone and get things percolating again. I waved goodbye and left, feeling confident things would proceed in a more positive manner.

The next morning I got an emergency phone call from the theatre. Damage control meeting immediately.

I was ushered into the boardroom. The director, Bob and Dobbin were all there. Everyone was very serious. Susan felt I'd seriously undermined her work yesterday when I'd burst into rehearsal and taken it away from her.

I explained that, after weeks of actor hell, I really felt I had no choice but to address the issue in the rehearsal space as that's where most of the turmoil seemed set. I only did the blocking exercise with the actors because the director seemed preoccupied at the time and the performers desperately needed something to hang on to.

Susan felt I no longer trusted her with the play. She was right and I told her so. I told her that it appeared that the majority of people involved in the play didn't trust her work, despite the fact they wouldn't admit it. I told her I was still at her disposal but, as far as trust went, she'd have to earn that back.

Rehearsals resumed. I stayed well away, determined not to venture anywhere near the theatre for the final rehearsal period. After two days the then-lover came home from rehearsal and broke down into tears. Things had gotten worse since my visit. Nothing had changed. The actors were trampling all over themselves, each other and the play because it had no control track holding it together.

The lead actress called me to tell me that she had no idea where she was going or what she was doing and wanted to quit the show.

The lead actor called. He'd had it as well. All the other shows were going so well and everyone hated working on *Remains*.

I lost it. I had a bit of an hysterical fit, swearing that if the theatre was going to hurt this much to work in I couldn't work in it for very much longer. Nothing was worth this kinda shit. I really indulged myself. I even got the then-lover to forget his own whining for a moment.

The next day I unexpectedly turned up at rehearsal. I greeted everyone pleasantly and took a seat at the back of the bunker and watched as the actors stumbled through something approximating a run.

It was shit. A director and a group of actors apologizing for everything they were doing and saying while they said and did it. It was unwatchable. Everyone acted as if they were playing the villain in a Disney film. The light, human moments of the show were rendered nonexistent by the overbearing darkness of everything else.

I had emergency meetings with Bob White and Kathy Allison, the show's dramaturge, and explained my misgivings. Both, busy directing other shows and dealing with their own traumas, assured me that everything would work out if I minded my business and trusted Susan.

If I remember correctly Michael Dobbin was too busy with the show he was directing and the general running of the theatre to see me at all.

It became clear that I was on my own.

No problem. Warnings had been given.

I dropped back into rehearsal to watch Susan rehearsing with the lead actress. The actress was so clearly baffled by whatever it was the director was trying to get across that it was painful to watch her face as she listened. The other actors loitered around looking exasperated.

Then it hit me.

Everyone had become afraid of the play.

The rehearsal process had become such a forum of justification and apologia for everything the characters did in *Remains* that no one in the show remembered the laughter and fun at the initial reading. They'd been taken too far in another direction and now each actor seemed to be stumbling through some self-absorbed murk that denied the action of the play and any true contact among the characters. Some of them had started the process by disliking the director. Now many of them were starting to dislike the play.

A kind of group hysteria had set in. Their internal performer fears were pitched at such a level that no matter what you said to these actors they heard "The play's shit. Everyone's going to hate you." We were doomed.

That night the lead actress phoned me to bitch about the director. I listened sympathetically and then gave the actress directorial advice I knew completely contradicted Susan's. I spent a long time on the phone with the actress, telling her more and more about Candy's character. Then I rang off and went to sleep.

Even though I'd just broken one of the cardinal rules of the theatre, a rule that states a writer must never contradict a director's direction when the director isn't around, I fell guiltlessly into sleep.

I'd broken every rule I'd been taught while I was writing the play. It sort of made sense that I'd have to break some rules in production as well.

When the then-lover called the next afternoon to inform me Susan was quitting the show and I was in deep shit around the theatre, I was only mildly surprised. He suggested I get my ass to the theatre ASAP. I took my time dressing and enjoyed a leisurely walk to the theatre. I pretty much knew what was coming. There was no need to rush.

The lead actress had gone into rehearsal that morning and started to alter what she was doing based on her conversation with me the night before. When the director stopped her to question what she was doing, the actress said that the playwright had told her to do this and it seemed to work a lot better.

Susan left rehearsal, walked to the administration offices and announced her resignation as the director of *Unidentified Human Remains and the True Nature of Love.*

The theatre went into an immediate frenzy. A problem they'd all hoped to ignore had ignited in their faces. This was unprecedented. And it was only days until opening.

Emergency meetings were called. People who'd been far too busy to deal with the problem in an earlier stage suddenly found themselves pulled out of technical rehearsals to deal with this crisis.

I sat in the green room with the actors. We all knew what was going down. The actors seemed unable to decide whether taking sides would be wise. Everyone knew there was trouble and all were doing their best to avoid being implicated in any way.

A silence had fallen over the building. The only movement was that of Bob and Susan in the main office with Dobbin. I kept expecting to be summoned, asked to explain, asked to apologize, but the call never came. Some hours later Bob simply walked into the green room and announced that Susan was leaving the show. She had just left the building. I was asked to follow him to Dobbin's office.

Both Dobbin and Bob were suitably neutral and nonjudgmental, although they made it clear they questioned the professionalism of my conduct. I shrugged and told them I did what I felt I had to do to save my play. Dobbin spoke fleetingly of cancelling the show. I told him that was fine with me. I didn't want the show seen in the shape it currently was in. It was decided that Bob, whose show opened a week before *Remains,* would take over the direction. I continued to offer my advice to those actors who asked for it. Any specific notes I had went through Bob.

The actors suddenly had a focus. Between Bob's competent connection to problem areas, my suggestions, some of Susan's detailed character work in the early part of her process, and their own instincts, which they were learning to trust again, the show started to come together.

Elsewhere in the theatre things were seething. A contingent of Brad-haters had their tongues wagging about how awful I'd been to the poor director of my show. When Susan had her name removed as director of the show a number of other artists did the same in support of her. Because of this, the wonderful welded metal set was never properly credited. This is too bad because it was the focus and challenge of the set that pushed the actors into the dangerous playing level the play needed.

Finally, in the last hours of a torturously long technical rehearsal, the actors claimed the play in a way that combined their work with Susan and Bob and myself and things really started to cook.

The final run through terrified everyone. There was a power in the show that seemed to roll from the stage in waves. We were all desperate to see how an audience would react.

Our first preview was a fundraiser for a Calgary AIDS hospice and a battered women's shelter. We couldn't have tailored a better first audience if we'd tried.

What I remember most from that first performance is the symphony of laughter and silence that the audience formed to underscore the play. It sounded exactly as it had in my head. Small giggles of provocative shock building to snorts and short bursts of laughter, building to rollicking waves with an undeniable current of their own. If my plays were dance tunes the laughter would be the percussion track that holds all the softer bits together. The actors, thrown by the volume of comedy they were discovering in the play, had sounded a few false notes, but I knew these would pass after a performance or two.

We were an immediate sellout. Martin Morrow, theatre critic for the *Calgary Herald*, was one of the play's earliest and most vocal supporters. His trumpeting of the play's virtues must have had something to do with the way the phones in the box office started ringing off the hooks. But the big seller was word of mouth—and word around town was that *Unidentified Human Remains and the True Nature of Love* was something worth seeing.

Despite the warning signs all over the theatre, and someone from the theatre coming out just before curtain and offering to refund the audience's money if anyone wanted to leave, people called up in droves wanting tickets to "that play about love and broken bones" or "the one with the naked people." Every performance was S.R.O. within days of opening.

For me it was all a bit surreal. I'd been an hour late on opening night, thanks to that particularly Calgarian phenomenon called too-much-snow-not-enough-taxi-cabs, and finally ended up watching the show on the television monitor in the green room. I've often watched my plays this way. It makes them easier to study objectively. Also, sometimes watching them in the theatre just becomes too much. I become too aware of shifting in seats, unfolding legs, blowing noses and all those assholes with wracking coughs that should have stayed at home.

The impact of the play's success never really hit me until I showed up for the last performance. A lineup of people had formed at the box office hoping for no-shows and last minute cancellations. As I walked past them a few people I didn't know called out my name and exhorted me to find them tickets. I shrugged apologetically and continued into the theatre.

It was the closing weekend of the festival, called the Blitz Weekend because theatre folks from all over the country show up to see a reprise of all the festival's plays. This gives the whole closing weekend a strangely inverted opening feel because of the calibre of people present and the growth the plays have seen. *Remains* was the hot ticket and, love it or hate it, everyone had something to say about it. As I moved through the lobby to the theatre I could feel people watching me. People I didn't know kept smiling at me. It was fucking weird.

I ducked into the theatre and immediately went up to the darkest, farthest corner of the top balcony. This is my favourite place to watch my plays because the show I see doesn't just exist on the stage but spills out into the house as well. For me the audience is an indispensable part of the show. I have to see them while I see the play.

At the end of the first act, after the audience had applauded too hard and too long, I watched a middle-aged couple who'd been sitting in front of me rise to stretch their legs. They looked like the parents of all the middle-class friends I had when I grew up. The man turned to the woman and said, "Not bad eh? Not bad for one of them plays. Funny." The woman nodded in agreement. I noticed there was a strange, almost stoned, glassy look to her eyes. She said, "I like it a lot."

At that moment something in my life changed in a way I still can't define. But I knew something had just opened up for me.

The Play Gets a Life

Despite the hit status of the show in Calgary there wouldn't be another production until later next season. I went back to work as a waiter and spent a large portion of the summer playing Stratford wife to the then-boyfriend who was doing his requisite young actor time on the Bard ride. I wrote *The Ugly Man*. Also, the then-lover and I cobbled together a zippy adaptation of *The Revengers Tragedy*, shortly to be directorially slaughtered by the then-artistic director of Northern Light Theatre.

Finally the Crow's Theatre production of the play opened in Toronto under the direction of Jim Millan. This production was most notable for its exceptional acting, particularly Lenore Zann as Candy and the incandescent Brent Carver as David. It was an immediate sellout in the tiny Poor Alex Theatre and would later be revived, ironically enough, at the much larger Theatre Passe Muraille, where both *Wolfboy* and *Young Art* had bombed earlier.

My own production in Edmonton opened shortly after the Toronto production and became the highest grossing show Workshop West had ever produced. It was later revived for a longer run at the Roxy Theatre where, in another of those ridiculously convenient coincidences that dog my life, I had worked as an usher while I was in high school. It had been a second-run movie theatre at the time and I wrote my first plays leaning over the candy bar while the some foreign soft-core porn film played to the usual fourteen people.

A French production at Theatre Quat'sous, directed by the highly esteemed André Brassard, caused a sensation in Montreal and caught the attention of Denys Arcand, who would go on to direct the film adaptation.

It was about this time my then-boyfriend and I split up. We both knew life was taking us in different directions and we allowed it to happen.

A Chicago production did a respectable commercial run despite the rather sniffy, paternalistic reaction of the closety American press. They were not impressed by my attempts to bring the language of popular culture into the theatre.

On the other hand, the experience of the Chicago production was one of the best I'd ever known. Director Derek Goldby did an excellent job and the actors were a wonderful, warm bunch. We were all from out-of-town (a fact that was eventually to work against us with the press and local theatre types) and were put up in this huge old hotel. The inclement weather and the gruelling rehearsal schedule, coupled with the fact that everyone was desperately working out because of the nude scenes, meant that we all spent a lot of time together, mostly smoking dope and playing celebrity. I remember this time and this particular cast with great warmth.

When we got the production to New York six months later, the mood had changed considerably. People felt there was a lot more at stake and certain actors had already been replaced. We were playing the Orpheum, a quality off-Broadway house. All the actors had new demands and conditions. The producers were looking more and more stressed. I was rushed from interview to interview by a very friendly and very efficient publicist who had two dogs the size of small rats. Everything was fast and hard. Everyone involved with the show had their eccentricity buttons turned up full. It was as if the heat and stench of New York in August brought out the diva in them all.

I tried not to buy into any of it, keeping a very neutral Doris Day sort of attitude. Besides, I had other things to cope with. Like my drunken pigslut friends who showed up to party in New York and kept dragging me out until all hours. One of them contracted salmonella poisoning from a turkey sandwich at a late-night deli and nearly died in my apartment as hordes of people from Edmonton converged on NYC for the hometown boy's opening, all of them bearing gifts and flowers. The period leading up to opening and opening night itself was like the gay version of a family wedding.

It was an amazing time and an amazing experience. Opening night was a tizzy of celebrities, drag queens and flashbulbs. I remember everything perfectly up until the point where I was smoking something out of a glass pipe with some people I didn't know in a washroom I didn't remember and then it gets rather hazy.

The next day, after a rudely early CBC radio interview, a bunch of us were sitting around the dumpy-with-character apartment the producers had rented for me on the edge of Hell's Kitchen. The reviews had come out. They were mixed but generally positive. Beers were opened. Joints were being passed around. My plane back to Edmonton was to leave in a couple of hours. The telephone rang. I picked it up. It was *Time* magazine calling to get the correct spelling of my name and my birth date. I could barely contain myself. You know you've arrived somewhere when *Time* calls you.

The New York production of *Remains* only ran for three and a half months. It never showed a profit to my knowledge and the producers stopped paying my guarantee shortly after opening. This money was never completely paid to me and because of that the producers lost any other ownership they might've had in the property.

It seemed as if the *Remains* ride was over. The well had dried up and it was time to get onto the next project. You can't be the next big thing if you haven't got a big thing to show them next.

Then something really interesting happened.

Remains went international.

First it was produced by the Traverse Theatre in Edinburgh in tandem with the Hampstead Playhouse in London. The production was an unqualified hit, winning me both the *Time Out* Award and the *London Evening Standard* Award for most promising playwright. I put these awards on the mantle along with the Chalmers Award and Sterlings the show had already won.

Suddenly, I found myself being invited to Milan or Berlin or Tokyo for productions of the show. I wasn't able to take advantage of all these invitations, but the few I could schedule were very illuminating. The Italian production is a particular standout. The theatrical style was something between performance art and high opera. It was fascinating and wonderful and I was pleased to discover that the play lived just as happily in that milieu as it did with North American naturalism. In fact, no matter in what language I've seen the play, it always works pretty much as it always has: with laughs, gasps and screams falling in pretty much the same place, no matter what culture composes the audience.

The play has been produced in Sweden, New Zealand, Australia, South Africa, Poland and innumerable amateur and especially student productions all over North America. Other than the movie, I've had very little to do with the play since it left North America. It's like a wonderful child that has grown up and struck out for a life on its own, only this child sends frequent cheques home from its travels.

What I Think Now

Unidentified Human Remains and the True Nature of Love changed my life. Literally. It took me from one particular world into a quite different one. I've lost and gained friends, family and lovers because of events the play was a catalyst to. I've been able to support myself solely as a writer since the show opened and have, over the last few years, begun to make quite a nice living at my chosen profession.

Remains may well be the kind of play that comes along once in a writer's lifetime. On the rare occasions that I glance back to it now, I'm always amazed at the play's rawness and vitality and I'm always vaguely embarrassed by the clumsiness of some of the writing. I've since gone on to write better plays, but I've never exploited the power of the theatre in such an exciting way. I think that has a lot to do with the conflict the play was born out of: from the conflict in my life and my feelings about the theatre, to the conflict in the lives of the people around me, to the conflict in the first rehearsal period, to the conflict in the press and within the theatre community itself about the script's merits and shortfalls. *Remains* has always generated an energy of its own that's much larger than any one personality, playwright included, could hope to spark.

I think this is a testament to the power of collaboration that is the backbone of exceptional theatre. After all, the essence of drama is conflict. Wouldn't it be naive to believe that something as dramatic as *Remains* would be born without some conflict among the people creating it? To all those people who took part in the conflict that created this play, some named in this introduction and some not—they know who they are—to all those people I say thank you. Your contribution was enormous. Perhaps we all made mistakes but we are all human. And we all learned something.

I regret none of it.

Brad Fraser
January 16, 1996

An Explanation of the Changes

The old adage goes "If it ain't broke don't fix it." I'm a firm believer in this particular platitude and the changes that I've made to the script after nearly twenty years of success weren't undertaken lightly.

For a long time I resisted altering the play in any way. But as time moves on and things change the theatre, which captures the tenor and zeitgeist of the immediate moment in a way no other medium can, may become very dated. Slang, pop culture references and even profound societal concerns can fall out of popular awareness in a way that cannot be foreseen or controlled. Because of this any play can find its shelf life seriously curtailed after a relatively short period of time.

Luckily that has never happened with this play. New generations keep discovering the show. It speaks to them in the same way it spoke to mine, but not in quite the same language. Things that were very cutting edge at the time, like answering machines, are now all but extinct and some of the topical issues no longer resonate. Further, a lot of people have asked me if they could change the locale of the show in order to make it more pertinent to their own environment; therefore there have now been productions where the play takes place in New York, Sydney or Denver. I've allowed this to go on because, frankly, there's really nothing I can do about it. Reinventing plays is standard procedure with any classical text and seems inevitable to most works that will enjoy a prolonged popularity. Because of this, when I was approached about allowing changes to the script for a new production in London, I finally decided to take the bull by the horns and produce a script free of the indicators that keep it too firmly fixed in space and time in hopes of standardizing the many "adaptations" that have been finding their way onto stages all over the world.

The show is still set in Edmonton but producers are encouraged to change specific place names—and place names only, please don't mess with the dialogue—to reflect the city of their own choice. The answering machines have been replaced by cell phones and voice mail, although I have no doubt they will someday need to be reinvented again. This script keeps the story and characters intact with very few alterations while still maintaining a language of its own. Of course, there were points where I couldn't resist cleaning and editing a bit, but such changes are very small and the essential fabric of the show remains untouched.

The title, too, has been changed. Some may question the wisdom of this but the truth is, over the years, that's how everyone, including me, has come to refer to it. I don't think your average theatre-goer will even notice any of these alterations—including the original title which only I ever got right anyway. However, for those who feel that Cindy Lauper's remake of "Girls Just Want To Have Fun" and George Lucas's re-polishing of the first *Star Wars* movies were a mistake, have no fear. The original version of *Unidentified Human Remains and the True Nature of Love* still exists as a script and people are free to produce whichever version they prefer.

Brad Fraser
August 30, 2006

Love and Human Remains, (Unidentified Human Remains and the True Nature of Love), was first produced by Alberta Theatre Projects for the playRites '89 New Play Festival, with the following company:

DAVID	John Moffat
CANDY	Ellen-Ray Hennessy
BERNIE	Peter Smith
KANE	Jeffrey Hirschfield
ROBERT	David LeReaney
JERRI	Wendy Noel
BENITA	Kate Newby

Lighting Design by Steve Isom
Costume Design by Pamela Lampkin
Sound Design by Allan Rae
Fight Director: Jean-Pierre Fournier
Director: Fate

Characters

DAVID
CANDY
BERNIE
KANE
ROBERT
JERRI
BENITA

Setting

Any city like Edmonton, Alberta, Canada. Various locations.

Production Note

During the course of the action, none of the actors should leave the stage unless absolutely necessary. The play is written with a secondary score used to create a background to the main action, as indicated in the stage directions. Intermission, if desired, is indicated.

LOVE AND HUMAN REMAINS

Blackness. Pools of light appear on each character.

DAVID Skin.

CANDY Blood.

BERNIE Breasts.

KANE Hair.

ROBERT Feet.

JERRI Hands.

A light on BENITA.

BENITA The case of the headless boyfriend. That's a good one. This girl and her boyfriend are driving to their high-school prom. They're all dressed up and everything—but they're late—right? So they're taking this back road—and all of a sudden they run out of gas. The guy tells the girl to wait in the car. He's going to go back and get help. She doesn't want to, but she's in her high heels and everything so she says she'll wait. But she's scared.

JERRI Alone.

BENITA So the guy tells her to get into the back seat and cover herself with a blanket and not to come up until he knocks on the window to get in.

ROBERT Dark.

BENITA She locks herself in and does what he said—and she waits and waits and waits for him. Then, a long time later, she hears this sound. She thinks it's him. Knocking for her. So she peeks out from under the blanket and can't see anything. But the sound's still there and it's like this tapping.

KANE Wet.

BENITA But she can't see where it's coming from. So she hides back under the blanket and stays there all night. Crying.

BERNIE Dying.

BENITA Finally, in the morning there's a knock on the window. She looks out. There's a cop there saying, "Step out of the car and come with us Miss."

CANDY Why?

BENITA He tells her not to turn around. She walks to the cop car but she can't stand it any longer and she turns around and looks.

DAVID No!

BENITA Her boyfriend's hanging from a tree above the car. He's been skinned and his head's been cut off. The tapping she heard was the sound of his blood dripping on the roof of the car all night. They had to put her in a nuthouse for the rest of her life. My mother told me that story. She said it happened to a friend of hers when they were girls.

DAVID When I think of skin I think of Candy.

CANDY The sun.

DAVID Lying back. Little blond hairs sticking out of the skin around her navel. I think of Bernie.

BERNIE He's back.

DAVID When we were camping. So hot that day. The brown of his skin made the hair on his chest blond. I think of Dana. Candy.

CANDY Flesh.

DAVID Bernie.

BERNIE Come.

DAVID Dana.

CANDY Blood.

DAVID Jesus!

BENITA sings softly as lights rise on the apartment.

BENITA Lavender blue dilly dilly
Lavender green
When I am king dilly dilly…

DAVID enters.

DAVID Honey! I'm homo.

CANDY rushes to him.

CANDY Darling!

They fake kiss.

DAVID I feel like I just fucked a football team.

CANDY Good money?

DAVID A hundred. Not bad. If you like serving food. Going out?

CANDY No. I've got this book to review. *Teach Me How to Love* by Linda Carlyle.

DAVID Tell tell.

CANDY It's about a poor American girl who moves to New York and makes it big in the fashion industry.

DAVID Original!

CANDY How do you drag out the phrase "It's shit" to seven hundred words?

DAVID You'll find a way.

DAVID moves to his room to change.

CANDY Where are you off to?

DAVID Out and about.

BERNIE alone.

BERNIE My bro.

CANDY Bernie called. It's on the machine.

DAVID Put it on the speaker.

CANDY turns on the telephone speaker. We hear BERNIE.

BERNIE *(on machine)* Hi big guy. Just called to see what you're up to after work. I'm at the office. Gimme a call.

DAVID What time is it?

CANDY Just after midnight.

DAVID Call him tomorrow. You wanna come to Flashback with me? We can wear all our tightest things.

CANDY Too tired. Did you see the paper today?

DAVID Nope.

CANDY They found another girl.

The other characters are isolated.

BENITA Mutilated.

JERRI Bleeding.

KANE Cut.

BERNIE Dead.

DAVID Where?

CANDY The ravine on Eighty-Second.

DAVID Jeez.

CANDY That's two this month.

DAVID enters from the bedroom, changed. He presents himself to CANDY with a flourish.

DAVID Well?

CANDY Stunning. Fabulous.

DAVID I have a blind date with destiny.

CANDY Be careful.

DAVID Always am. You eat today?

CANDY A bit.

DAVID Eat something.

CANDY I will.

DAVID Later.

CANDY Ciao.

A light on KANE.

KANE I can't remember the name of the show, but I remember him. He was the best. Then he came to work here.

The restaurant. KANE is eating his dinner. DAVID is doing his cash out.

Good night?

DAVID Three hours, seven bottles of wine, four course, and they leave me ten percent on the total. Fucking peasants!

KANE Bogus huh?

DAVID You don't look Californian.

KANE Huh?

DAVID Never mind.

DAVID finishes his cash. He starts to leave.

KANE I remember you. From this show.

DAVID No you don't.

KANE You played this rebellious kid. Named Toby.

DAVID You've confused yourself.

KANE You're David McMillan—right?

DAVID Discovered again.

KANE Do you still do—you know—TV stuff?

DAVID It's called acting. And no—I don't.

KANE Why not?

DAVID I find being a waiter more artistically satisfying.

KANE You don't do it at all?

DAVID No. I drink a great deal and sleep around. It pays better. I've got tables to set.

DAVID exits. The characters speak from the darkness.

CANDY Food.

JERRI I don't even know her and I can't stop thinking about her.

CANDY I'd barf.

JERRI Her hair.

CANDY I need to go out more.

DAVID It's the same. Everything's the same. I go to the club —the music's the same. The faces are all the same. The price of drinks is the same. Sal says he's slept with everyone worth sleeping with. Rod says he hates this fucking town. Sal wishes he were in Toronto. Murray talks about all the people we never see out anymore. I play pinball and drink more beer.

CANDY There's this spot on the futon. It looks like grease or something. I hate finding spots on the futon.

JERRI Her hair.

KANE His face.

BERNIE David.

DAVID Later I walk home.

JERRI Empty.

DAVID Pissed to the tits. Some car follows me down Jasper Avenue. I give up in front of a twenty-four hour store and stop—get into the car.

BENITA Mutilated.

DAVID He drives for a while then pulls into the parking lot by the parliament buildings and sucks me off. I shoot into his mouth and he swallows it.

BENITA *(sings)* Lavender blue dilly dilly…

DAVID enters the apartment.

CANDY There's a spot on the futon.

DAVID I'm fuckin' bushed.

CANDY Get lucky?

DAVID Got blown. What kinda spot?

CANDY I dunno. Look.

DAVID I'd guess either pizza or Vaseline.

CANDY Where'd it come from?

DAVID How should I know? Mebbe someone broke in when we weren't home and rubbed pizza on our futon. Who cares? We'll get it cleaned.

CANDY I hate it.

DAVID I worry about you darling—you need to get out more—sleep around a bit.

CANDY With the men in this town?

DAVID Now now. We have some fine men.

The other men are isolated.

BERNIE Fire.

KANE Dark.

ROBERT Cold.

CANDY I need someone who'll hang around for my orgasm.

DAVID Then stop dating straight men.

CANDY Maybe I'd have better luck with women.

DAVID I dunno, Candy, I can't see you as a dyke.

CANDY Please. I'd be a lesbian.

DAVID I'm starving. Any old food hanging around?

CANDY Don't be stupid.

DAVID How 'bout a medium Rose Bowl pizza with pepperoni, green peppers and anchovies?

CANDY I'd sooner drink piss. See you in the morning.

DAVID If I haven't wasted away by then.

CANDY You'll live.

CANDY waves at him and exits to her bedroom. DAVID switches on the TV and stares at it blankly. A light on ROBERT alone.

ROBERT Evelyn had this thing about feet. The first time I met her she said it was my feet that attracted her. I should've known then that things wouldn't work out.

The apartment. DAVID alone staring at the TV.

DAVID The dream. I buy this baby on sale at Kmart. Only it doesn't have any arms or legs—just little flipper things and nubs where its limbs should be. Its head's covered with purple booga things and its jaw doesn't close right. Sometimes its stomach bursts open and these slimy clockwork guts fall out. It can talk—sort of—but all it ever says is "I love you David. I love you."

There is a knock at the door.

Yes?

BERNIE It's me. Bernie.

BERNIE enters. His face is covered with blood and he is very drunk. He practically falls into DAVID's arms.

DAVID Bernie.

BERNIE Hey pal.

DAVID examines BERNIE's face.

DAVID How's it goin'?

BERNIE Good, but there's blood all over my face.

DAVID Just a minute.

DAVID gets a cloth to wipe BERNIE's face as they speak.

BERNIE Not interrupting anything, am I?

DAVID Never.

BERNIE How are you?

DAVID Great. You reek.

BERNIE Beer or Scotch?

DAVID Scotch.

BERNIE Good. I hate it when I smell like beer.

DAVID I know exactly what you mean. No class. What happened?

BERNIE Jealous husband.

DAVID Bernie.

BERNIE Came home early. Sucker got me right in the nose. Why didn't you call me back?

DAVID 'Cause I hate your fucking guts.

BERNIE Good. I thought you were avoiding me. Gotta crash.

DAVID Want me to call Linda?

BERNIE No! I'll call her in the morning.

DAVID Sure.

BERNIE You mean a lot to me, David.

DAVID Bernie, what a lovely thing to say. Want me to suck your cock?

BERNIE Ha ha. Good night, David.

BERNIE exits to the bedroom.

DAVID Good night, Bernie.

The others speak from dim light.

KANE Too hot.

JERRI Can't sleep.

ROBERT Alone.

BENITA's place.

BENITA What about this one? This guy and his girlfriend are parked in a lovers' lane necking and petting when a special report comes on the radio and says that there's an escaped killer in the neighbourhood and everyone should stay inside and lock their doors and windows because the guy's crazy and he's got a hook where his hand used to be. Well, of course the girl's real scared and wants to leave right away, but the guy's got a bone on and doesn't want to stop until the girl gets good and mad and says if he won't drive her home she'll get out and walk. So he gets pissed off and slams the car into gear and tears off, real abrupt, calling the girl a chicken and all that. When they get to her place he hops out of the car and goes around to open her door for her. Then all of a sudden this big guy screams, turns white and faints. The girl thinks "What the hell?" and gets out. When she closes the door she sees a bloody hook hanging from the door handle. That's a good one.

The apartment. BERNIE and DAVID are sleeping. DAVID is undressed and under the covers. BERNIE is dressed and on top of the covers. BERNIE's cell phone rings, waking DAVID. DAVID finds the phone in BERNIE's pocket and answers it.

DAVID Hello? Hi. Yeah. Sure. Hang on.

DAVID shakes BERNIE.

It's your wife.

BERNIE grabs the phone from DAVID.

BERNIE Linda. Honey. Sorry! Yeah. I should've called. David and I got too drunk—

DAVID Hey.

BERNIE Didn't want to drive. I'll be home soon. Yeah. Me you too.

BERNIE hangs up.

DAVID David and I got too drunk?

BERNIE C'mon.

DAVID I won't be an easy excuse for you.

BERNIE David—

DAVID Keep it up and I'm gonna start demanding sexual favours in return.

BERNIE You wish. Shit!

DAVID What?

BERNIE I'm late for work.

DAVID See how God punishes you for lying.

ROBERT alone.

ROBERT It's like this white ball of flame that starts building at the back of your head. It's hot and it makes this kind of vibration, like someone screaming—but there's no sound.

DAVID Call in sick.

BERNIE Could.

DAVID Of course you could. You work for the city.

BERNIE Don't rub it in.

DAVID Did you shit in my mouth while I was sleeping?

BERNIE It was the only way to stop your snoring.

DAVID You should talk. At least I didn't throw my arm over your shoulder every five minutes and dig my erection into the small of your back.

BERNIE I didn't do that.

DAVID You did.

BERNIE Gotta piss.

BERNIE exits the bedroom, nearly running into CANDY, who is dressed for the gym.

Heya Candy.

Pause.

Quiet this morning. Not feeling well…?

CANDY Fuck off.

DAVID enters.

DAVID Candy?

CANDY exits.

BERNIE Still hates my guts.

DAVID Dana was her best friend.

BERNIE She killed herself. I didn't do it.

DAVID Let it go.

The gym. CANDY is working out. JERRI is watching her.

JERRI You look great.

CANDY Thanks.

JERRI I watch you.

CANDY finishes her set.

CANDY I know.

JERRI extends her hand to CANDY.

JERRI Jerri.

CANDY shakes JERRI's hand.

CANDY Candy.

JERRI I think we're in the same stretch class too. You're amazing.

CANDY I like to keep in shape.

JERRI Can I spot you?

CANDY Sure.

The apartment.

BERNIE Christ, you smoke a lot.

DAVID You cheat on your wife.

BERNIE Hey!

DAVID Sounded like a criticism to me.

BERNIE You see the paper? They identified that girl they found in the ravine.

BENITA alone.

BENITA Cold eyes.

BERNIE Sally Wilson. Sixteen. Sexual assault and mutilation. Details are being withheld.

DAVID I'm sure it's never as bad as we imagine.

BERNIE You think it's wrong? The way I fool around on Linda.

DAVID None of my business.

BERNIE It just kinda happens.

DAVID I can relate to that.

BERNIE I know.

DAVID Difference is—I didn't get married.

BERNIE I did.

DAVID I know.

The gym.

JERRI Thighs?

CANDY Thighs are hard. It's diet as much as exercise.

JERRI Jiggly underarms?

CANDY Tricep extensions. Dips.

JERRI Breasts?

CANDY Bench press. Flyes.

JERRI You do all this stuff?

CANDY Four times a week.

JERRI You must be very hard.

CANDY I'm working on it.

The apartment.

BERNIE That whole time you were away—I missed you.

DAVID Bernie, are you trying to get real with me before we've even cleaned the snot out of our eyes?

BERNIE Naw.

DAVID Something on your mind?

BERNIE Why's everything so hard?

DAVID I don't know.

BERNIE It seems like—no matter how hard you work—no matter what you do—it's never enough.

DAVID Bernie, it's ten a.m. You got something smaller on your mind?

BERNIE No.

The bar. ROBERT is working. CANDY enters.

ROBERT Hey gorgeous—the usual?

CANDY Soda water—double lime.

ROBERT gives her the drink.

Thanks, guy.

ROBERT My pleasure.

CANDY Pretty slow.

ROBERT Yeah, but we'll be packed with secretaries in another hour. Want a chicken wing?

CANDY No thanks.

ROBERT They're free. Happy hour.

CANDY No.

ROBERT You—uh—you ever drink anything besides soda water?

CANDY *(smiles at him)* Occasionally.

The apartment. DAVID and BERNIE.

BERNIE Let's go up to LaRonde and drink daiquiris all afternoon.

DAVID I'm trying to cut back.

BERNIE On LaRonde?

DAVID On daiquiris.

BERNIE You're getting boring, David.

DAVID It's my age.

The bar. CANDY and ROBERT.

CANDY Why do you ask?

ROBERT Because I'd like to take you out sometime.

CANDY I hardly know you.

ROBERT You will if we go out.

CANDY You could be some kind of sicko.

ROBERT You see me here every day.

CANDY It's always the ones that seem the most normal that turn out to be axe murderers.

ROBERT I'm no axe murderer.

CANDY Promise?

ROBERT Promise.

CANDY I'm free Thursday.

JERRI on her cell phone.

JERRI Hi Candy, this is Jerri. The person from the gym. I got your number from the membership list. I hope you don't mind. I thought I'd call and see what time you're coming to workout tomorrow. We can have coffee or something. I'll call back.

The restaurant. DAVID is doing his cash. KANE is eating.

KANE Good night?

DAVID Rang eight fifty.

KANE All done?

DAVID Yep.

KANE Got plans?

DAVID Not really.

KANE Wanna go for a beer or something?

DAVID With you?

KANE If you want.

DAVID Sure.

BERNIE alone. CANDY alone.

BERNIE The graveyard.

CANDY Dana.

BERNIE I took him there when the acid kicked in. The headstone kind of glowed in the dark. I heard him breathing and thought he might understand.

CANDY Dana.

A bar. DAVID and KANE are drinking beer.

DAVID So if you're so loaded how come you work as a bus pig.

KANE Nothing else to do. Besides, I'm not loaded. My dad is.

BERNIE alone.

BERNIE I thought he might understand.

KANE You're gay huh?

DAVID Not professionally.

KANE Gay's cool.

DAVID I'm glad you approve.

KANE How old are you anyway?

DAVID Thirty in a few months.

KANE Really? You don't look older than twenty-seven.

DAVID Thanks.

KANE You're in great shape for your age.

DAVID It's the Geritol.

KANE Wanna go for a pizza or something?

DAVID Why not?

JERRI alone.

JERRI I cook for myself. A lot of people don't like to, but I don't mind. I usually cook up a week's meals in advance then freeze them. It's cheaper than eating out every night.

KANE's car.

DAVID Thanks for the ride.

KANE No problem.

DAVID Wanna come in?

KANE To your apartment?

DAVID For a beer or whatever.

KANE My dad doesn't like it when I stay out too late.

DAVID How old did you say you were?

KANE Eighteen.

DAVID And you've still got a curfew?

KANE His house—his rules—you know?

DAVID No. But I'll take your word for it. Tomorrow.

KANE You bet.

ROBERT alone.

ROBERT She's the one.

KANE alone.

KANE I was given this car and its insurance when I turned sixteen. I got a Visa card when I was seventeen. My dad owns a Mercedes and a '62 Corvette convertible. We have a kidney-shaped pool and a Winnebago. Sometimes I dream I have worms in my scrotum.

The apartment. CANDY and DAVID.

CANDY This bartender wants to take me out.

ROBERT alone.

ROBERT Control it.

DAVID Hold out for a brain surgeon.

CANDY He's hot.

DAVID You're so shallow.

CANDY It's either him or the lesbian I met at the gym.

DAVID Take the bartender. Mixed marriages seldom work.

CANDY I'm half tempted.

DAVID The lesbot? Darling, one doesn't seriously discuss changing their sexual orientation at thirty—people lose respect.

CANDY I need some tenderness in my life.

DAVID Pick the lesbian.

CANDY I want more than just sex.

DAVID That's why God invented the movies.

CANDY The bartender's quite nice.

DAVID Candy, you're talking about a date, not a lifetime commitment.

CANDY Don't you ever wish you had a lover?

DAVID I have many lovers.

CANDY Not lover lovers.

DAVID Puh-lease!

CANDY Everybody needs somebody.

DAVID Need I remind you there was a time that you and I were lovers.

CANDY That was different.

DAVID We had nothing but sex in common.

CANDY Don't you ever see someone and it's like this thing goes off in your head and you just want to be with them all the time?

DAVID No.

CANDY Deep down you want someone to be special for you.

DAVID I'm quite capable of being special for myself. What you're talking about doesn't exist, Candy.

CANDY What about my parents?

DAVID Your parents are the Macbeths in normal clothes.

CANDY You're wrong, David. It's love. Two people going completely gaga over each other.

DAVID You watch too much television.

CANDY David, you need to be loved.

DAVID I have my friends.

CANDY It's not the same.

DAVID Are you saying my relationships with you and Bernie are invalid?

CANDY Bernie? Right. He's psycho.

DAVID Candy…?

CANDY I saw the blood on the face cloth.

DAVID He was in a fight.

CANDY That's healthy?

DAVID Let's not discuss this. You've always hated him.

CANDY Because he's weird, David. Weird.

DAVID Drop it.

CANDY Do you love him?

Brief pause.

DAVID He's my friend.

CANDY Do you love me?

Pause.

DAVID That's not the right word.

CANDY You love me.

DAVID There's no such thing.

CANDY I know you love me.

DAVID Then why do you have to ask.

Pause.

CANDY I'm going to bed.

DAVID Good night.

CANDY exits.

ROBERT, KANE and BERNIE alone.

ROBERT Some men have it.

BERNIE Some men control it.

KANE Some men understand.

The gym. CANDY and JERRI.

JERRI I hope you don't mind me phoning like that. It's kinda forward—I know—but sometimes if you don't make the first move with people nothing happens.

CANDY I don't mind.

JERRI It's not really like me really. It's just—I haven't been here very long and I don't know anyone.

DAVID alone.

DAVID Love.

CANDY It's all right.

JERRI So, do you want to go out or something sometime?

CANDY Sure.

DAVID Bullshit.

JERRI When?

CANDY Well—uh—whenever.

JERRI Should I call you?

CANDY Sure.

JERRI Why don't I give you my number then you can call me too—if you want.

CANDY Why not?

JERRI Great.

The bar. DAVID and KANE are playing with a Gameboy as they drink.

KANE It's the patterns.

DAVID Patterns. Gotcha.

KANE Just like last time. The spaceships always come out of the left, then the right, then straight up the centre. All you gotta do is shoot them. Just watch me.

JERRI alone.

JERRI This time.

DAVID You ever read, Kane?

KANE Sometimes. Not much. See those things—those wavy things—don't get caught between them or you're toast.

JERRI Please.

DAVID Where's your mother?

KANE Hawaii.

DAVID They divorced?

KANE Naw. She just likes to tan a lot. Your parents here?

DAVID They're both still out in Beverly.

KANE Beverly?! You're from Beverly and you're a homo?

DAVID Yeah. You got a girlfriend?

KANE I did for a while, but we broke up when she went to university.

DAVID Why?

KANE Because—because she went to university.

DAVID Of course.

BERNIE enters the bar.

BERNIE There you are.

DAVID Grab a seat. Have a beer.

BERNIE I dropped by the restaurant. They said you were probably here.

KANE Bonus stage. Stay centre and keep firing.

DAVID Bernie, this is Kane. Kane, my brother Bernie.

KANE Hi. Your brother? You don't look like brothers.

DAVID Jesus, Kane, you don't have to be related to someone to be their brother. *(to BERNIE)* Right?

BERNIE Right.

A loud beep from the machine.

KANE Shit! I'm dead.

BERNIE Lucky.

ROBERT's place. CANDY is drinking white wine.

ROBERT Was dinner okay?

CANDY Fine.

ROBERT You didn't eat much.

CANDY It was lovely.

ROBERT So you review books.

CANDY Yes.

ROBERT How is it?

CANDY Okay. I don't finish most of them. They're generally drek.

ROBERT Is that fair?

CANDY Probably not.

ROBERT You're a very interesting woman.

Long pause. CANDY turns and looks at ROBERT.

What?

CANDY Nothing.

CANDY picks up a trophy and looks at it.

What's this?

ROBERT Fly-fishing trophy.

CANDY How butch.

ROBERT Would you like to go sometime?

CANDY No. I loathe the outdoors. Too many bugs.

ROBERT Oh. I'll put some more music on.

ROBERT puts on something soft and romantic.

More wine?

KANE alone.

KANE It's the patterns.

CANDY I'm fine.

ROBERT Would you like to smoke a joint?

CANDY No.

ROBERT Oh—uh—would you—

CANDY *(cutting him off)* Do you want to fuck me?

Pause.

ROBERT Sure.

CANDY Not right now though.

ROBERT It's late.

CANDY I'll go.

ROBERT Wait.

CANDY I shot your little game down and blew it. Sorry. The soft and romantic thing doesn't really work for me.

CANDY exits.

ROBERT Shit.

The bar. KANE and BERNIE watch DAVID playing the video game.

KANE Left. Left!

There is a loud beep from the machine.

DAVID Damn! Killed again.

KANE You're catching on.

DAVID I think my attention span's too well developed for this.

CANDY at the apartment.

CANDY Why did I do that?

BERNIE I'm outta here.

DAVID Already?

BERNIE Things to do.

DAVID Keep your nose in one piece this time.

BERNIE Later.

BERNIE exits.

KANE He gay?

DAVID No.

The apartment. CANDY is picking up her voice mail on her cell.

JERRI *(on phone)* Hi Candy. It's me. Jerri. Just calling sometime like I said I would. Wanted to see if you're still interested in getting together for whatever. You've got my number. Why don't you give me a call?

CANDY hangs up.

CANDY No way.

Pause.

Well—maybe.

Pause.

No way.

JERRI alone.

JERRI Please.

KANE and DAVID at the bar, no longer playing video games.

KANE Another jug?

DAVID You trying to get me drunk and take advantage of me?

KANE Should I?

CANDY at the apartment.

CANDY No way.

DAVID What do you think?

JERRI alone.

JERRI She'll call.

KANE What was it like, being on TV?

DAVID Okay. Good money.

KANE You were famous.

DAVID Slightly.

KANE I always wanted to see you on another show.

DAVID I did try. Even moved to L.A. for a while.

KANE Why'd you come back here?

DAVID This is home.

KANE You miss it?

DAVID L.A.?

KANE TV.

A short pause.

DAVID No.

The apartment. CANDY on her cell.

CANDY Hello. Jerri. It's me. Candy.

JERRI alone.

JERRI Yes!

KANE and DAVID at the bar. The lights come up.

KANE Jeez—they're closing already.

DAVID Sure are.

KANE Now what?

DAVID Isn't it after your curfew?

KANE He's out of town.

DAVID You feeling adventurous?

KANE Adventurous how?

DAVID I could take you for an adventure right now.

KANE Like on TV?

DAVID Better.

KANE What?

DAVID C'mon.

KANE Where?

DAVID takes KANE's hand and leads him out of the bar.

DAVID Trust me.

CANDY, JERRI and ROBERT in isolation.

CANDY Oh boy.

JERRI Thank you.

ROBERT Shit!

BENITA's place.

BENITA *(alone)* What about the one about the babysitter and the extension phone? The babysitter's babysitting, alone, on a stormy night when the phone rings. It's some guy and he says, "I've killed once and I'm going to kill again." She hangs up and freaks out. Locks all the doors and windows. Then the phone rings again—

BENITA is interrupted by a knock at the door.

Anyway, the guy was upstairs on the extension the whole time. He killed all the kids. Yes?

DAVID *(off)* It's me.

BENITA opens the door. DAVID and KANE enter. BENITA kisses DAVID.

BENITA Honey, how are ya?

DAVID Drunk. You?

BENITA Can't bitch.

DAVID You're—uh—not busy are you?

BENITA It's fine.

DAVID Meet my newest friend. Kane.

BENITA This is a first.

KANE falls onto the bed.

DAVID Also my drunkest friend.

BENITA Charmed.

KANE I'm not drunk.

BENITA You want me to read him.

KANE Whaddya mean, "read me."

DAVID She's psychic.

KANE Right.

BENITA I'm sensitive. I see stuff in people.

KANE What stuff?

DAVID Relax.

BENITA *(to DAVID)* You sure you want me to do this?

DAVID He's up for it. *(to KANE)* Right?

BENITA Looking good, Davey.

KANE Davey?

DAVID She's the only one who gets away with that.

As they speak, BENITA gets a small baggy of white powder from a drawer. She cuts the powder into lines on a mirror.

Kane's my bus boy.

KANE He's famous.

BENITA Why don't you dump this waiter shit and come work with me?

DAVID Little long in the tooth for that, Benita.

KANE What's she doing?

BENITA offers DAVID a line.

BENITA Davey?

DAVID No thanks.

BENITA Not in the market anymore?

DAVID I'm clean.

BERNIE alone.

BERNIE I'm clean.

BENITA Good.

BENITA takes the mirror to KANE.

This is for you.

KANE Is that coke?

BENITA It'll loosen you up.

KANE I don't wanna be loose.

DAVID It's okay.

KANE David...?

DAVID We'll find out what's inside you.

KANE There's nothing inside me.

DAVID It's okay.

KANE She gonna read you too?

BENITA Can't. He's got a block.

KANE Mebbe I've got a block too.

BENITA Fat chance.

KANE Hey, how old are you anyway?

DAVID Just one snort.

KANE I will if you will.

Short pause.

DAVID All right.

DAVID sniffs a line. KANE sniffs a line.

KANE That was coke, wasn't it?

BENITA Junk.

KANE Heroin?! I don't do heroin!

DAVID puts his arms around KANE.

DAVID It's okay.

KANE Feel sick.

DAVID It'll pass.

KANE I don't like it.

DAVID I won't let anything bad happen to you.

KANE gets a rush and lies back on the bed.

KANE Oh.

BENITA Where did you get him?

DAVID He followed me home.

KANE Dad…?

BENITA He's very cute.

BENITA touches KANE. DAVID takes her hand away.

DAVID Do it.

Short pause. BENITA lays her hands on KANE's forehead and sings quietly to herself.

BENITA Lavender blue dilly dilly
Lavender green
When I am king dilly dilly
You shall be queen…

KANE moans softly. BENITA closes her eyes. All other characters are seen in dim light.

CANDY Dana.

JERRI The wind.

CANDY I found her body.

BERNIE I drive.

CANDY She didn't leave a note.

ROBERT The night.

CANDY She would've left a note.

JERRI The dark.

CANDY She would've left a note!

BENITA draws quickly away from KANE. She is agitated.

DAVID Well…?

KANE Feels nice.

BENITA Give me a minute.

KANE Dolphins.

BENITA Swimming pool.

KANE Whales singing.

BENITA Cars. Credit cards. Video. Pink and blue. Men and women. Men. A man. Older. Glasses. Moustache. You.

DAVID Me?

BENITA But smaller. Video.

DAVID The show.

BENITA Your face superimposed over the man's. Your voice. Your hands. Loneliness. Fear.

Short pause. BENITA takes a breath and calms down.

Fear.

DAVID That's it?

BENITA He's only seventeen.

DAVID He told me he was eighteen.

BENITA He lied.

KANE We're here. Right?

BENITA He's fried.

KANE You're a movie star. Right?

DAVID Thanks, Benita.

BENITA He really is cute.

DAVID Go ahead. He's all yours. Got any beer?

BENITA pulls up KANE's shirt and caresses his chest.

BENITA In the fridge.

DAVID exits to get beer. BENITA undoes KANE's pants and strokes his cock. KANE moans in pleasure. DAVID enters with a beer and watches as BENITA takes KANE's cock in her mouth.

Booze and junk and he still gets hard.

DAVID Seventeen.

BENITA sucks off KANE. DAVID, BERNIE and CANDY are singled out by separate spots.

It was the acid.

BERNIE He was scared.

DAVID I ran out of the graveyard because I was peaking and I didn't like thinking about her.

BERNIE I thought he might understand.

DAVID But Bernie wouldn't let me go.

BERNIE I thought.

DAVID He wouldn't let me go.

CANDY Dana?

KANE comes with a loud moan. The lights return to normal.

DAVID That was quick.

BENITA Seventeen.

DAVID offers BENITA some money.

DAVID Here.

BENITA Keep it. I'll get you to do something for me sometime.

DAVID You're on. He lied to me.

BENITA Everyone lies.

DAVID Yeah?

BENITA He loves you.

DAVID There's no such thing.

BENITA He doesn't know that.

DAVID *(quietly)* No.

DAVID exits. KANE is still oblivious.

KANE David.

Lights fade to black. There is a loud, terrified scream from a woman. It is drowned out by the sound of a vacuum cleaner, very loud. Lights rise on the apartment. CANDY is vacuuming and singing very loud.

CANDY Aphids on roses and nipples on kittens
Sleigh balls and snow balls and fat nylon mittens
Bright stupid packages tied up with string…

DAVID enters from the bedroom.

DAVID Candy.

CANDY *(can't hear him)* These are a few of my favourite things.

DAVID *(yells)* Candy!

CANDY turns off the vacuum, very startled.

CANDY David?!

DAVID It's nine o'clock in the morning for Christ's sake.

CANDY I couldn't sleep. Tea's still hot. David, our floors are a mess.

DAVID helps himself to tea.

DAVID We'll get to them.

CANDY They're filthy.

DAVID They're floors. People walk on them. It's unavoidable.

CANDY They found another girl last night.

DAVID What a charming way to greet the day.

CANDY You should see all the hair I swept off the bathroom floor.

DAVID Too much stress in our lives.

CANDY I'll say. This city's getting scary.

DAVID I'll say.

CANDY Why don't they ever find men raped and mutilated?

DAVID Men don't complain about it.

CANDY What about that guy they found who'd been mutilated and dumped in a septic tank. That was really weird.

DAVID Yeah. But he wasn't complaining.

CANDY We really do have to get after these floors.

DAVID When it snows.

CANDY I dread the thought of another winter here.

DAVID Why? It's only ten months.

CANDY begins to dust.

CANDY You—um—working tonight?

DAVID I always work Saturday nights. You know that. Why?

CANDY Just wondering.

DAVID Having someone over?

CANDY What makes you think that?

DAVID You're acting weird.

CANDY I enjoy cleaning.

DAVID Who is it? The bartender?

CANDY No.

DAVID Not the dyke!

CANDY Quit calling her that.

DAVID It is the dyke.

CANDY David.

DAVID I don't believe it.

CANDY I'm warning you—

DAVID Carpet munching in my own home.

CANDY Shut up!

Pause.

DAVID Kidding.

CANDY Shut up!

The restaurant. KANE alone.

KANE You ever have one of those dreams where you're the only one in the whole restaurant, when all of a sudden it fills up with people and you have to cook all the food and make all the drinks and wait on everyone?

DAVID enters.

DAVID Comes with the territory.

KANE That girl the other night—?

DAVID Benita.

KANE She really read my mind?

DAVID What little there was.

KANE No way.

DAVID Your dad has a moustache and wears glasses.

KANE Cool.

DAVID You also lied to me about your age.

Pause.

KANE I'm nearly eighteen.

DAVID It doesn't matter. What's on the agenda for tonight?

KANE I—I sorta made other plans.

DAVID Other plans?

KANE I told this person—this girl—I'd meet her.

DAVID Ah.

KANE Just a friend.

DAVID Whatever.

KANE I didn't think you'd mind.

DAVID I don't.

KANE Sure?

DAVID Sure. I'm outta here.

KANE Tomorrow?

DAVID Whatever.

The apartment. CANDY and JERRI are drinking martinis.

CANDY Hoo, is that ever strong.

JERRI You want me to throw another olive in it?

CANDY I'll manage.

JERRI Anyway, so I left him. Just packed my things and said "Sorry, you're not my type," and left.

CANDY That's why I like living with David. He's gay but he doesn't treat me like I'm from Mars or something.

JERRI Some people are freaked out by gays.

CANDY In this day and age. Can you believe it?

DAVID on his cell.

DAVID Hi bro. I seem to be without an escort tonight and thought you might like to get stinky. Call me.

CANDY and JERRI. The apartment.

JERRI You're the kind of person other people watch. So focused.

CANDY It's the only way to get anything accomplished.

Pause.

Did you find out you were lesbian after you got married?

JERRI I knew. I just fought it.

CANDY You'd like to sleep with me, wouldn't you?

JERRI Very much. But it's okay if we don't.

CANDY I can't say I haven't thought about it.

JERRI I know.

Pause.

Candy?

CANDY Yes?

JERRI I love you.

Pause.

CANDY Ah.

DAVID alone.

DAVID I do all the usual shit at Flashback—drink until the place is closed, avoid the eyes of all the ugly men who want me, dance, get bored, leave.

ROBERT alone.

ROBERT They're not like us.

DAVID on the street.

DAVID It's warm. I start thinking about Victoria Park and even though I tell myself that I won't go—that it's scary and it's dangerous—I know I will.

JERRI and CANDY. The apartment.

JERRI I'll go if you want.

CANDY No.

JERRI I've made you uncomfortable.

CANDY Yes.

JERRI I've loved you from the first time I saw you.

CANDY No.

JERRI Something just went off in my head and I wanted to be with you—all the time.

Pause.

Say something.

CANDY Our floors are a mess.

DAVID in the park.

DAVID It's dark. The wind's blowing. You can hardly see anything when you get into the trees.

KANE alone.

KANE Maybe tomorrow.

DAVID But you get used to the dark. Cigarettes glow. Someone coughs. Someone clears their throat. Someone moans.

KANE Maybe someday.

DAVID I follow the path. Moonlight on the leaves.

CANDY and JERRI. The apartment.

JERRI Relax. It's not like I'm gonna kill myself if you're not into it.

CANDY Did you read about that girl the other day?

JERRI But I do want to touch you.

CANDY It's horrible.

JERRI Your skin. Your hair.

CANDY Raped and mutilated.

JERRI Candy?

CANDY Give me a minute.

The phone rings. CANDY starts to move toward it.

JERRI Leave it.

CANDY picks up the phone.

CANDY Hello? Pause. Hello? *(pause)* They hung up.

DAVID in the park.

DAVID I smell the leaves rotting. Bodies moving around me. Someone reaches out and touches my crotch. I lean against a tree and light a cigarette.

CANDY and JERRI. The apartment.

JERRI You look scared.

CANDY Me?

JERRI I won't hurt you.

CANDY suddenly moves to JERRI and kisses her on the lips. JERRI puts her arms around CANDY.

DAVID in the park.

DAVID Sometimes, when I come down here, I think about what it would be like if I stumbled across a dead guy on these paths. I'm following some humpy number deeper into the bushes when my foot hits something soft.

BERNIE alone.

BERNIE David?

The apartment. CANDY and JERRI undress and begin to make love.

DAVID Like a rotten log. Only it's not a log. It's some dead boy. Some dead boy with moss growing in his hair and maggots living in his eye sockets. It could happen. This is the perfect place for it.

The characters are singled out by spots.

CANDY Dana.

BERNIE The abortion. I remember Dana telling us. David and I'd been camping. Her and Candy were waiting for us.

DAVID Candy.

KANE David.

BERNIE We'd just gotten out of the truck. David was carrying the rifle. I was carrying the one partridge we'd managed to bag that weekend.

DAVID Someone approaches me. He smells of cigarette smoke and Clorets. I stand perfectly still as he undoes the buttons of my fly. I unroll the condom and slide it onto my dick. He pulls his pants down and grabs a tree. And while I'm fucking his ass the same stupid song keeps running over and over in my mind. "Billy, don't be a hero, don't be a fool with your life. Billy, don't be a hero…"

CANDY and JERRI in bed. CANDY comes quite vocally.

JERRI You needed that.

CANDY Yeah.

JERRI It's not the same as with men, is it?

CANDY No.

JERRI reaches out to CANDY. CANDY pulls away and slides out of bed.

I need a minute.

BERNIE The abortion.

JERRI Not too long.

CANDY Just a minute.

CANDY, DAVID and BERNIE are singled out by spots.

I think of David and Bernie and Dana.

BERNIE Dana.

CANDY The four of us.

BERNIE David.

DAVID Bernie.

CANDY Dana.

DAVID Candy.

CANDY We did everything together.

DAVID Partying.

CANDY Drinking.

BERNIE Fucking.

DAVID Friends.

CANDY She tells me.

DAVID We're camping.

BERNIE Hunting.

CANDY She cries.

BERNIE He's cold.

CANDY Doesn't know what Bernie will say.

BERNIE I want to tell him to get into the sleeping bag with me.

CANDY I hold her.

DAVID I want to tell him.

BERNIE But I can't.

CANDY Her parents will kill her.

DAVID But I can't.

BERNIE I hear him breathing in the dark.

CANDY She's scared.

BERNIE He's scared.

DAVID Bernie. I think I'm queer.

BERNIE Ha ha.

DAVID I am.

BERNIE Go to sleep.

CANDY Dana. Laid back on some kind of metal table. Metal things jammed into her cunt. Is there blood? Does it hurt? Did she cry?

BERNIE I pretend to sleep.

DAVID I whisper into the dark.

CANDY She's in the waiting room. White.

DAVID *(whispers)* I love you.

CANDY She won't look at me.

DAVID Bernie?

CANDY We watch them get out of the truck.

DAVID I know he heard me.

BERNIE They're waiting for us.

CANDY David looks terrible.

BERNIE It's like they know something.

CANDY Bernie's hurt him too.

BERNIE The one partridge we managed to bag that weekend swings in my hand.

CANDY I stare at Bernie.

BERNIE Dana stares at the bird.

CANDY He looks at her like she's something dirty.

BERNIE The bird stares at nothing.

CANDY Walks right past her.

DAVID Something's wrong with Dana.

CANDY You asshole!

BERNIE Get off my back.

CANDY It was your baby!

BERNIE What did you want me to do? Marry her?

CANDY Yes!

BERNIE I—didn't—love—her.

CANDY You pig!

BERNIE Fuck off!

DAVID Stop it.

CANDY I found her.

DAVID We were kids.

CANDY The razor beside the bed. Her sheets covered in blood.

DAVID Candy—don't…

CANDY The smell.

JERRI Come to bed.

BERNIE She was weak.

CANDY I'm coming.

DAVID I'm coming.

BERNIE I'm coming.

ROBERT Candy.

KANE David.

DAVID The guy straightens up. His shirt's plastered to his back with sweat. I can't see his face. He whispers something, I don't know what, and walks away.

BERNIE And the dirt falls onto her coffin a handful at a time.

DAVID Bernie.

BERNIE David.

CANDY Dana.

DAVID Candy.

Blackout. There is a woman's terrified scream from the darkness. Lights up on BENITA's place.

BENITA Okay. Let's see.

DAVID *(off)* No.

BENITA Come on.

DAVID Benita—really…

BENITA Come on.

DAVID enters in a cowboy suit.

DAVID Darling, this really isn't my milieu, if you know what I mean.

BENITA You look real butch.

DAVID I *look* like one of the Village People.

BENITA You owe me, David.

DAVID All right. All right.

BENITA Just do like I told ya. When he comes in here and starts slapping me around you keep begging him not to hurt your little sister.

DAVID This guy wouldn't hurt you, would he?

BENITA Probably not.

The apartment. Morning. JERRI has made tea. CANDY enters, hungover.

JERRI Good morning.

CANDY Morning.

JERRI pours CANDY some tea. CANDY won't look at her.

JERRI Looks kinda chilly out there this morning.

CANDY Yes.

Pause.

JERRI You were pretty restless last night.

CANDY Nightmares.

Pause.

JERRI So—does it take you long to do these floors?

CANDY Yep.

Pause.

JERRI Well you've probably got a lot to do today.

CANDY Yes.

JERRI gets her coat.

JERRI Candy, it's weird for everyone the first time.

CANDY Sure.

JERRI Call me when you get over it.

JERRI exits.

BENITA's place. DAVID is removing the cowboy gear.

BENITA I read this book about Ed Gein—he's the guy they based *Psycho* and *Texas Chainsaw Massacre* on. Did you know they think he's killed at least fifteen women? That's all they can confirm. They think he might've eaten the rest.

DAVID Charming.

BENITA You wouldn't believe the stuff they found. Jewellery made outta fingers, clothes made outta skin, a heart on the stove, four noses in a tea cup.

DAVID Jesus, Benita!

BENITA I think he's still alive—locked up somewhere. I love reading about that kinda stuff.

They share a cigarette.

DAVID Is that healthy?

BENITA Is anything anymore?

DAVID Watching some guy abuse you for hours sure isn't.

BENITA Just think, Davey—if we hadn't been here to help him live out that fantasy he might've forced it on someone else—for free.

CANDY alone.

CANDY Fucked up.

DAVID He stared at me the entire time. He coulda been my father—your father.

BENITA My father was never that gentle.

DAVID Jesus.

BENITA How's it going with the middle-class white boy?

KANE alone.

KANE I don't know.

DAVID I don't know.

BENITA *(suddenly)* Hey! You got colours.

DAVID Huh?

BENITA I've never seen stuff like that around you before.

DAVID What is it?

BENITA Something—something dangerous.

DAVID For me?

BENITA Can't tell. Someone you love maybe.

DAVID Fat chance.

BENITA Be careful.

DAVID Okay. Daylight already.

BENITA Be careful.

DAVID Always am.

The bar. ROBERT is working. CANDY enters.

CANDY Hiya, guy.

ROBERT Candy—you're early today.

CANDY Decided to skip the gym.

ROBERT That's not like you.

CANDY Yeah. Well.

ROBERT hands CANDY a soda water.

ROBERT On the house. My way of apologizing.

CANDY I should do that.

ROBERT How 'bout if we forget the whole thing and start again?

CANDY How 'bout it.

The restaurant. KANE enters.

KANE Good night?

DAVID Yeah.

Pause.

KANE What'd you do last night?

DAVID Got drunk, fucked some guy in the park, dressed up like a cowboy and watched some old man abuse Benita.

KANE Oh. *(pause)* I had fun.

BERNIE alone.

BERNIE I had fun.

DAVID Good.

KANE If you want we could—

DAVID I'm meeting someone tonight.

KANE Oh. *(short pause)* Who?

DAVID *(exiting)* I don't know. I haven't met them yet.

CANDY and ROBERT in bed.

CANDY You got a condom?

ROBERT Yes. Wait. No.

CANDY Damn.

Short pause.

ROBERT I'm okay.

CANDY You sure?

ROBERT Promise.

CANDY Just this once.

They begin to fuck. ROBERT's phone rings.

ROBERT Shit.

CANDY You want to get it?

ROBERT checks the call display.

ROBERT No.

CANDY Good.

Lights on a rooftop downtown. DAVID and BERNIE are sharing a bottle of Scotch wrapped in a brown bag.

DAVID Look at that sky. You can't see a sky that endless anywhere else.

BENITA Yep.

DAVID Other places, there's always something in the way.

BERNIE Not all of us got to leave.

DAVID You could've come to visit.

BERNIE You could've come to my wedding.

DAVID I couldn't afford it.

BERNIE You were supposed to be my best man.

DAVID Don't.

Pause.

You ever feel like you've failed?

BERNIE Sometimes. You?

DAVID I'm a waiter.

BERNIE I'm not even sure what I do sometimes. I know it's got something to do with sanitation.

DAVID We had all those plans.

BERNIE You talk like things are over.

DAVID Not over. Different.

BERNIE At least you went somewhere.

DAVID L.A. Big deal.

Pause.

You happy, Bern?

BERNIE Right now?

DAVID Generally.

BERNIE Sometimes.

DAVID We're not the same.

BERNIE We're not kids anymore.

DAVID No. I mean *we're* not the same. I don't know you like I used to.

KANE alone.

KANE Don't think of him.

BERNIE You sayin' I've changed?

DAVID I dunno. It's not the same. What's this?

BERNIE What?

DAVID Right here. It fell out of your pocket. An earring? You doing drag, Bernie?

BERNIE takes the earring from DAVID.

BERNIE Linda's.

BERNIE moves to the edge of the rooftop.

DAVID Careful.

BERNIE Take my hand.

DAVID Why?

BERNIE Just take it.

DAVID takes BERNIE's hand.

Let's jump.

DAVID laughs and pulls away from BERNIE.

DAVID No way.

JERRI on her cell.

JERRI *(on machine)* Hi Candy. It's Jerri. Just wondering why I haven't seen you at the gym lately. You're getting soft. Call me.

CANDY and ROBERT in bed.

ROBERT Did you come?

CANDY It was great.

ROBERT Did you come?

CANDY Sure. I came.

ROBERT You're beautiful.

CANDY Thank you.

JERRI on her cell.

JERRI Hi Candy. It's Jerri. I've got an extra ticket to the symphony and thought you might like to come. Call me before seven.

DAVID and BERNIE on the rooftop.

BERNIE You know what I like best about coming up here?

DAVID What?

BERNIE You can spit on anyone walking by and they'll never know where it came from.

DAVID *(laughs)* Right.

BERNIE So what's happening with that Kane kid?

DAVID Nothing. You gonna stay married, Bernie?

BERNIE Linda "loves" me.

DAVID Do you love her?

Pause.

BERNIE I thought it would change things.

DAVID Did it?

BERNIE Nope.

BERNIE spits off the edge of the building.

JERRI on her cell.

JERRI It's Jerri. Just thought I'd call to see how you are. Why don't you give me a call?

KANE alone.

KANE Just call him.

JERRI Please.

ROBERT and CANDY in bed.

ROBERT I love your tits. I love your skin. I love your hair.

CANDY Mmm.

ROBERT Anything you love about me?

CANDY Everything. Your face. Your chest.

ROBERT What about my prick?

CANDY It's a great prick.

ROBERT Not too small?

CANDY It's fine.

ROBERT What about my feet?

CANDY Never noticed them. Sorry.

ROBERT Great.

JERRI on her cell.

JERRI Jerri. *(short pause)* Call me.

DAVID and BERNIE on the rooftop.

BERNIE I can't stop looking for women to bone.

DAVID I hope you're playing safe.

BERNIE Straight people don't get AIDS.

DAVID Don't talk stupid.

BERNIE Anyway, it's not such a big deal anymore.

DAVID It makes you sick and eventually kills you.

BERNIE You think about it that much?

DAVID I don't want to die.

BERNIE Nothing's any fun if the possibility's not there.

Pause.

DAVID You mean that?

BERNIE You useta feel the same way.

DAVID I've changed.

BERNIE gets up.

BERNIE We've all changed.

DAVID Heading home?

BERNIE Don't wanna upset Linda. Need a lift?

DAVID No. I'm going to the club.

BERNIE Later.

DAVID Later.

ROBERT's place. CANDY is dressing. She steps on something sharp and pulls it out of her foot.

CANDY Robert?

ROBERT enters in his underwear eating a sandwich.

ROBERT What?

CANDY I stepped on this earring.

ROBERT Let's see. You okay?

CANDY Fine.

CANDY hands him the earring. He examines it.

ROBERT Weird.

CANDY Whose is it?

ROBERT shrugs.

ROBERT I don't know.

CANDY You got someone else in your life?

ROBERT No.

CANDY Good.

The restaurant. DAVID is eating. KANE enters.

KANE Good night?

DAVID Mediocre.

KANE Wanna come to a poker game?

DAVID No.

Pause.

Please don't look at me in that tone of voice.

KANE What did I do?

DAVID Nothing.

KANE exits quickly. The apartment. CANDY, fresh from the shower with robe and towel, is listening to her messages on speakerphone.

JERRI I don't normally do this. But I can't seem to get you out of my mind. Is it getting weird?

DAVID enters the apartment. CANDY doesn't notice him.

If it is, I'll stop. I just don't understand—why won't you call me back?

DAVID clears his throat. CANDY turns the speaker off.

DAVID If you don't want to talk to her why don't you just call her and say so?

CANDY Because then I'd be talking to her.

DAVID Haven't seen much of you lately.

CANDY I'm in love.

DAVID I know. You've stopped living here.

CANDY I've been home.

DAVID Sure. Long enough to leave a ring in the bathtub and steal four of my condoms.

CANDY David, I think he loves me.

DAVID Great. Mebbe he'll clean the tub and replace my condoms.

CANDY You're cranky.

DAVID Slightly.

CANDY Get over it. We're having company.

DAVID Candy. No.

CANDY Darling, this is a potential future husband we're talking about.

DAVID Don't be stupid. Who'd marry you?

CANDY Lotsa people.

DAVID Like the psychotic cunt-bumper with the phone fetish?

CANDY Don't.

DAVID Did you actually…?

JERRI alone.

JERRI Yes.

CANDY Daaavid.

DAVID All right already.

DAVID moves to the bedroom and changes as they speak.

You tell this guy I take it in the face?

CANDY Yes.

DAVID Great. Should I wear a dress or my knee pads?

CANDY Just be yourself.

DAVID Which one?

There is a knock at the door.

Let the Dick of Death in.

CANDY It's too early.

CANDY opens the door. KANE is there.

KANE Hi.

CANDY Hello. David, the paperboy's here.

DAVID goes to the door.

DAVID Kane?

CANDY Kane?

DAVID Candy, my bus boy Kane. Kane, my roommate Candy.

CANDY and KANE shake hands.

CANDY Charmed.

KANE Can I come in?

CANDY Feel free.

KANE enters.

KANE This isn't a bad time or anything, is it?

DAVID Well, Candy's betrothed is about to arrive.

CANDY David, don't be silly.

DAVID Beer?

KANE Sure.

DAVID Grab a coupla beers, wouldya Candy.

CANDY Exiting. Yassuh.

Pause.

KANE Guess I shoulda called or something first.

DAVID Maybe.

KANE I thought we could talk.

DAVID This isn't a very good…

CANDY enters.

CANDY Your beer, boys.

DAVID Thanks.

Pause.

CANDY Excuse me. I've got to see if I can torture my hair into some kind of submission.

KANE Sure.

CANDY exits.

Nice girl.

DAVID Thanks.

Pause.

KANE Look—I know—like we plan stuff and everything, but—you know—like—other things come up.

DAVID Sure.

KANE Sometimes I just want to get laid.

DAVID Kane, if you're really straight why are you so self-conscious about it?

KANE Who blew me the other night?

DAVID Is that what this is all about?

KANE I don't remember much—okay.

DAVID It was me.

KANE No.

DAVID And you liked it. You did the same thing for me.

KANE Really?

DAVID Get out of here.

Pause.

KANE David?

DAVID Just go.

KANE moves to the door. DAVID speaks just as he is about to exit.

Is it that important?

Pause.

KANE You're my friend. I don't want you to be mad at me.

DAVID It was Benita.

KANE Really?

CANDY enters.

CANDY Ta da! Gorgeous. *(pause)* Bad timing huh?

KANE It's okay. I'm going. *(to DAVID)* Could we—you know—meet later or something?

DAVID We'll talk.

KANE When?

DAVID Soon.

KANE Promise?

DAVID Sure.

KANE exits.

CANDY Who was that?

DAVID We're not sure yet.

BERNIE alone.

BERNIE It's like a hunger.

CANDY and DAVID. Waiting.

DAVID Perhaps it's car trouble.

CANDY He only lives four blocks away.

DAVID Foot trouble?

There's a knock at the door.

CANDY You get it!

DAVID Get a grip, girl.

CANDY exits. DAVID opens the door with a flourish.

Prince Charming. *(pause)* Oh.

JERRI enters carrying a gift.

JERRI You must be David.

DAVID Must be.

JERRI I'm Jerri.

DAVID Of course you are.

JERRI Glad to meet you.

DAVID Oh Candy…

CANDY enters.

CANDY Jerri!

JERRI I saw your light on and thought I'd drop in.

DAVID How lucky. Tea? Beer?

JERRI I'm not interrupting anything am I?

DAVID Not at all.

JERRI Candy?

CANDY Well—no.

DAVID exits. JERRI hands CANDY the gift.

What's this?

JERRI A gift. For your birthday.

CANDY My birthday was six months ago.

JERRI I missed it. Open it.

CANDY Not right now.

CANDY sets the gift down. DAVID enters with beer for everyone.

DAVID All outta tea. A gift. How festive! *(gives CANDY and JERRI beer)* Here ya go.

JERRI Thank you.

They sit. Long pause.

DAVID So Candy tells me you're a lesbian.

JERRI That's right.

CANDY David.

DAVID I'm queer myself.

JERRI I know.

Pause.

DAVID Well, we seem to have exhausted that particular topic.

Pause.

You two must have a million things to talk about.

JERRI Well—yes.

DAVID Don't let me stop you.

CANDY I'm going to kill you.

DAVID So Jerri, what do you do?

JERRI I teach school.

DAVID How interesting. What flavour?

JERRI Elementary.

DAVID Thank God, I was so scared you were gonna say gym. Do you love it?

JERRI I like children.

DAVID I'm a waiter myself.

JERRI Candy tells me you used to be on TV.

DAVID Oh, for a minute. Being a waiter's much more interesting.

JERRI It takes a special kind of person to wait tables.

DAVID Certainly. Someone brain-dead.

JERRI It's very high pressure.

DAVID You have no idea. People ordering Thousand Island dressing on their Caesar salads. Some nights I can't sleep.

JERRI *(laughs)* Right.

DAVID *(exiting)* I need another beer. Jerri?

JERRI I'm fine. *(to CANDY)* He's fun.

CANDY Riots. What are you doing here?

JERRI I wanted to talk.

CANDY No.

JERRI Why?

CANDY I don't feel right about what happened.

JERRI I'm not proposing marriage. I just want to be friends.

DAVID enters with another beer.

DAVID Puh-lease! Propose marriage. It's what she's been waiting for all night.

CANDY Would you stop it.

DAVID Immediately. I'm outta here.

CANDY Really?

DAVID I'd love to hang around and see how all this turns out, but you two obviously need some time to yourselves. Nice meeting you, Jerri. Have another beer.

JERRI Thank you.

There is a knock at the door.

DAVID I'll get it.

DAVID opens the door. ROBERT is there.

Well hello and do come in.

ROBERT David?

DAVID You must be Rhonda.

ROBERT Robert.

DAVID Whatever. Oh Candy…

Pause.

ROBERT Hi. Sorry I'm late.

DAVID Beer?

ROBERT Thanks.

DAVID takes the full beer from JERRI and gives it to ROBERT.

DAVID There ya go, big guy.

ROBERT Thanks. *(to CANDY)* Sorry. I got a long-distance phone call and couldn't get away.

CANDY I see.

JERRI I'm Jerri.

ROBERT Nice to meet you.

ROBERT and JERRI shake hands.

DAVID Candy, can I get you anything?

CANDY I thought you were going out.

DAVID Now? Are you crazy?

ROBERT *(to JERRI)* Are you a friend of Candy's?

JERRI Yes. You?

ROBERT Yes.

JERRI Great.

ROBERT Yes.

Pause.

Nice apartment.

DAVID Candy loves to decorate things.

ROBERT This is a real nice tofu.

Pause.

DAVID Futon.

ROBERT What?

DAVID It's called a futon.

ROBERT Oh. *(short pause)* Whose present?

JERRI It's Candy's. For her birthday.

ROBERT It's your birthday?!

CANDY No!

JERRI I missed it.

ROBERT *(confused)* Oh.

DAVID I think it's a lovely sentiment.

ROBERT Aren't you going to open it?

JERRI Please.

CANDY I don't really want…

JERRI Please.

DAVID Come on, Candy.

CANDY No. Really.

JERRI thrusts the gift at CANDY.

JERRI Please!

CANDY No, I…

JERRI Please!

CANDY roughly knocks the gift from JERRI's hand.

CANDY I don't want the goddamn thing!

Pause.

DAVID Well—smell her.

CANDY Shut up!

JERRI picks up the gift and shakes it. It rattles.

ROBERT Is it broken?

JERRI I think so.

ROBERT Candy.

DAVID That wasn't very nice.

CANDY I didn't mean to.

JERRI It wasn't anything much. Just a—a meaningful little something I picked up one day when I was thinking of you.

ROBERT That's all right Jerri.

DAVID I think you should apologize.

Pause.

CANDY Jerri—I'm sorry. This just isn't a good time.

DAVID *(confidentially to ROBERT)* PMS.

JERRI I just wanted to talk to you.

CANDY I can't.

ROBERT The lady brought you a gift.

CANDY Robert, you don't understand.

ROBERT She's your friend.

CANDY She's not. We talked a few times. I had her over once!

JERRI How can you say that?

DAVID And the psycho drama starts now.

CANDY It's true!

JERRI We slept together!

CANDY *(to ROBERT)* Don't listen to her.

JERRI I love you.

CANDY You do not.

JERRI I think about you all the time. I don't know how to stop!

CANDY You're crazy.

JERRI Take your present.

CANDY I don't want the fucking thing!

JERRI I bought it for you.

CANDY I don't care!

JERRI I don't want it!

CANDY Neither do I!

DAVID What is it?

CANDY Shut up!

ROBERT Calm down!

CANDY Leave me alone!

JERRI This will come back on you! It will!

DAVID Girls, girls.

JERRI What we did was real!

CANDY It wasn't!!

Pause.

DAVID Jerri—I think you'd better go.

JERRI exits. A long pause.

Well, anyone for coffee or liqueurs?

CANDY Fuck off!

Pause.

ROBERT I think I'd better go. *(to DAVID)* Thanks for the beer.

DAVID No prob.

ROBERT exits.

Pause.

Oh Candy…

CANDY Do you ever get tired of being a professional faggot?

DAVID You can't blame me…

CANDY You're a loser, David. You turn everything into a joke so you don't have to face what a fuck-up you are.

DAVID Let's not do this now.

CANDY You have nothing and no one in your life.

DAVID You're upset.

CANDY You don't think past the next beer and the next fuck.

DAVID At least I'm honest about it.

CANDY You have nothing!

DAVID Neither do you!

CANDY I'm not afraid to try.

DAVID With anyone that comes along!

CANDY That guy might've loved me!

DAVID You're pathetic, Candy!

CANDY Fuck you!

CANDY exits.

DAVID Candy—wait.... Shit!

Pause. DAVID sits and raises his beer in a toast.

Here's to love.

BERNIE alone.

BERNIE It's like a hunger.

DAVID In all its many forms.

Lights rise on BENITA.

In all its many forms.

BENITA The Saint Bernard at the top of the stairs.

Lights rise on CANDY and BERNIE.

CANDY Fuck him!

DAVID Bernie.

BERNIE You have to feed it.

CANDY He's empty.

DAVID Bernie's always my friend.

BENITA alone.

BENITA The babysitter stays over every night because the mom works the graveyard shift. All the kids sleep in the basement.

DAVID It's late.

BENITA Every night the babysitter goes through the same routine. Tucks the kids in, checks under their beds, locks the windows, looks in all the closets, turns out the light at the bottom of the stairs, walks up the dark staircase, pats the Saint Bernard on the head, and closes the basement door.

There is a knock at the apartment door.

Then checks the rest of the house and goes to bed.

Another knock.

She wakes up with this real bad feeling.

DAVID Candy?

Pause.

BENITA She thinks about the kids. Goes through everything in her mind.

DAVID Who's there?

Another knock at the door.

BENITA Checked everything, turned out the light, patted the dog, closed the door.

DAVID Who's there?

Another knock. Louder. DAVID stands.

BENITA Something was wrong.

DAVID goes to the door.

She ran down the stairs. The dog was gone. The bedroom doors were open.

BERNIE falls through the door and into DAVID's arms. He is covered with blood.

The kids had their throats cut!

DAVID Bernie?!

BERNIE Hey bro.

BENITA Every one of them. Dead.

DAVID Are you hurt?

BERNIE Yeah.

BENITA The Saint Bernard was at the end of the hall. Sliced wide open.

DAVID Are you cut? What?

BERNIE Drunk.

DAVID What happened?

BENITA And pinned to the dog was a note.

BERNIE Fight.

DAVID Let me look.

DAVID pulls off BERNIE's shirt and examines his body.

BENITA And the note read…

DAVID Jesus, Bernie.

BENITA It read…

DAVID You're not cut.

BENITA "It's as easy to pat a man on the head as it is a Saint Bernard."

DAVID You're not hurt.

BENITA He'd been at the top of the stairs when she went to bed.

DAVID Not hurt at all.

BENITA And it was his head she'd patted.

DAVID Where did all the blood come from?

BENITA His head.

DAVID Bernie?!

BERNIE I love you, David.

Blackout. A woman's scream rises from the darkness and bubbles away.

Intermission if desired.

A telephone rings twice. BENITA sings as the lights rise. Once she has established the song, DAVID speaks over it.

BENITA Lavender blue dilly dilly
Lavender green
When I am king dilly dilly
You shall be queen
Call up your men dilly dilly
Bid them to start…

DAVID In the dream I stand alone in a field on the farm where my grandparents lived—the sky's blue like on TV and tall clouds move across it. The wind on my face gets colder and things grow dark. I'm naked—with an erection.

The others speak from the darkness.

CANDY David?

JERRI Candy?

KANE David?

ROBERT Candy?

BERNIE My brother.

DAVID And when I wake up all I think is his name. Bernie.

Sound of a telephone ringing. The apartment. DAVID is listening on his cell. BERNIE enters from the bedroom and watches DAVID on the telephone.

BERNIE Who ya callin'?

DAVID hangs up quickly.

DAVID No one. Tea?

BERNIE Love some.

DAVID pours tea.

DAVID Where's Linda, Bernie?

BERNIE Home. Why?

DAVID I just called your place. You've had the same message on your machine for weeks now.

BERNIE *(shrugs)* Haven't changed it.

DAVID She's never home when I call.

BERNIE She's probably—you know—shopping or something.

DAVID Right.

Pause.

BERNIE Christ am I hungover. I haven't blacked out like that in years.

DAVID I thought you'd had your throat cut or something.

BERNIE Where're my clothes?

DAVID Hamper. What happened?

BERNIE Fight. Bad one. Don't remember much of it.

DAVID For fuck's sake, Bernie.

Pause.

BERNIE Linda left me.

DAVID What?

BERNIE Over a month ago.

DAVID Why?

BERNIE Things've been crazy. I drink too much.

DAVID Why didn't you tell me?

BERNIE I didn't think she meant it.

DAVID You should share that kinda shit.

BERNIE I deserve it.

DAVID Don't talk like that.

BERNIE Last night—I don't remember much—I was at the Crest—talking to some babe—then four guys were comin' at me.

CANDY alone.

CANDY Everyone lies.

DAVID The Crest?!

BERNIE There was a fight—someone pulled a knife—someone got cut—the cops showed up and the place went crazy.

DAVID You weren't holding the knife were you?

BERNIE No. I got out of there as fast as I could.

DAVID Good thing.

BERNIE Things get so goddamn strange. *(pause)* I don't even miss her.

DAVID It was a mistake. We all knew that.

BERNIE What did you know? You didn't know shit! You were too busy trying to be a fucking movie star!

DAVID I don't understand you, man.

BERNIE I gotta get to the office.

DAVID Take the day off.

BERNIE I can't take the fucking day off! I have responsibilities —obligations!

DAVID Okay! Don't take the fucking day off!

Pause.

BERNIE Can I borrow your blue tie?

DAVID Why not? I never wear it.

ROBERT's place. There is a knock at the door. ROBERT opens it. CANDY is there. Pause.

CANDY Hate me?

ROBERT No.

CANDY enters.

You look tired.

CANDY I stayed at my parents' last night. I hate that.

ROBERT I'm off to work. Why don't you lay down for a while.

CANDY Love to. *(short pause)* Robert, I'm ashamed.

ROBERT It was pretty weird.

CANDY Those things she said—

ROBERT Candy, we've all got our own stuff, right?

CANDY Right.

ROBERT I've gotta run. Let's talk after work.

CANDY Sure. Ciao.

ROBERT exits. The telephone rings.

DAVID alone.

DAVID Bernie.

CANDY calls to ROBERT.

CANDY Robert. Damn.

CANDY hesitates then answers the phone.

Hello. He just left. Candy. I'm a friend of his. You're who? O-okay. I'll tell him you called, Evelyn.

The restaurant. DAVID is doing his cash but seems to be having trouble concentrating. KANE enters.

KANE Good night?

DAVID Yeah.

KANE Hope you're tipping your bus boy well.

DAVID How's that?

DAVID gives KANE money.

KANE Great. Thanks.

DAVID You did good. We were really in the shit for a while there.

KANE Sure were. *(short pause)* You—uh—wanna do something tonight?

Pause.

DAVID Yes.

KANE Great.

ROBERT's place. CANDY lies on the bed. ROBERT enters trying to be quiet.

CANDY I'm awake.

ROBERT Couldn't sleep?

CANDY Evelyn called. She loves you and wanted to thank you for the lovely conversation you both had while I sat at my place and waited for you. She wants you to call Suzy.

ROBERT Evelyn's my wife. Suzy's our daughter.

CANDY I guess this makes us even.

The rooftop. DAVID helps KANE up.

KANE Pretty high.

DAVID It's one of my fave places.

KANE Did you hear they found another girl yesterday?

BENITA alone.

BENITA Cold eyes.

DAVID No.

KANE Think we got one of those serial killers?

DAVID Sure. What ever happened to all the people that used to come downtown?

KANE They go to the mall now.

CANDY and ROBERT.

ROBERT I care for you a lot.

CANDY Really?

ROBERT We've all got our own stuff.

CANDY You lied to me.

Pause.

ROBERT I love you.

CANDY No you don't.

JERRI alone.

JERRI I do.

ROBERT Yes I do.

CANDY No.

JERRI From the first time.

ROBERT From the first time you came into the bar. Something just went off in my—

CANDY Shut up!

DAVID and KANE.

KANE I want to be twenty-five. I'll understand stuff better.

DAVID Emotionally speaking, you've experienced everything you can by sixteen—everything after that's just a variation on a theme.

KANE Don't say that!

CANDY and ROBERT.

ROBERT I love you.

CANDY Don't say that.

ROBERT It's true.

CANDY It'll make things different.

ROBERT Too late.

CANDY I know.

DAVID and KANE.

DAVID Hold my hand.

JERRI alone.

JERRI She's scared.

KANE What?

DAVID You heard me.

KANE Why?

DAVID Because it's important someone hold my hand right now.

KANE takes DAVID's hand.

JERRI It's real.

KANE I'm—uh—not very comfortable with this.

DAVID I don't care.

CANDY and ROBERT.

ROBERT Look at me.

CANDY No.

ROBERT I said look at me!

ROBERT grabs CANDY and turns her to him, very hard.

KANE and DAVID. DAVID lets go of KANE's hand and steps out onto the roof ledge.

KANE What the hell are you doing?

DAVID Better view up here.

KANE You're crazy.

BERNIE alone.

BERNIE I'm clean.

DAVID extends his hand to KANE.

DAVID Come on up.

KANE No way.

DAVID Come on.

KANE It's too high. We'll fall.

BENITA alone.

BENITA Lavender blue dilly dilly
Lavender green
When I am king dilly dilly…

DAVID and KANE speak under BENITA's singing.

DAVID I won't let you fall.

KANE I don't know.

DAVID Take a chance.

BERNIE laughs. KANE takes DAVID's hand and steps onto the roof.

KANE It's scary.

DAVID If it's not scary it's not worth doing.

BERNIE laughs again, quietly.

KANE Some view.

DAVID Close your eyes. You'll feel like you're flying.

KANE I'll fall.

DAVID moves behind KANE and puts his arms around him.

DAVID I won't let you fall.

KANE That's pretty close.

DAVID Trust me. Close your eyes.

KANE closes his eyes. Pause.

KANE Cool.

DAVID pulls KANE back onto the roof.

DAVID Toldya.

CANDY and ROBERT.

ROBERT Tell me you love me.

CANDY No.

ROBERT You love me.

CANDY You lied to me.

ROBERT I was going to tell you.

CANDY Yeah? When?

ROBERT When the time was right.

CANDY When was that gonna be?!

ROBERT About the same time you told me about your fucking girlfriend!

CANDY You prick!

ROBERT Dyke!

ROBERT hits CANDY in the face. CANDY flies at him.

CANDY You prick! You fucking prick! I'll kill you!

ROBERT grabs her arms to restrain her.

ROBERT Candy—I'm sorry.

CANDY Fuck you!

CANDY breaks away from him and runs off.

ROBERT I love you.

BENITA alone.

BENITA After Ted Bundy was convicted of murdering thirty girls and women, he had dozens of proposals of marriage from women all over the world. Dozens.

The apartment. DAVID is there. CANDY enters, dishevelled and upset.

DAVID Candy…?

CANDY Don't.

Pause.

Asshole.

DAVID Snatch.

DAVID takes CANDY into his arms. She cries.

CANDY He hit me.

DAVID Oh baby...

CANDY Why's everything so fucked up?

DAVID Religion.

BERNIE alone.

BERNIE Being married's like being a grizzly in the zoo. If you don't have to hunt all you can do is pace.

Blackout. The characters are singled out on their cell phones.

ROBERT Candy, I'm sorry. Call me.

JERRI It's Jerri. Call me.

KANE David, call me.

BERNIE Call me.

JERRI Call me.

KANE Call me.

ROBERT Call me!

The apartment. DAVID and CANDY are cleaning. CANDY enters holding a bloody T-shirt.

CANDY Where's this bloody shirt come from?

DAVID It's Bernie's.

CANDY Bernie's?

BENITA alone.

BENITA Bernie's.

DAVID He left it here the other night.

CANDY What night?

DAVID I dunno. Friday.

CANDY Where'd all the blood come from?

BENITA The razor beside the bed.

DAVID He was in a fight.

CANDY What kinda fight leaves this much blood?

DAVID A fight where someone has a knife.

CANDY A knife?

BENITA Her shirt covered in blood.

DAVID At the Crest. Over some girl.

CANDY That's what he told you?

DAVID Yeah. What's the deal?

BENITA Bernie.

CANDY Let's call the Crest.

DAVID What?

CANDY Let's confirm his story.

DAVID You're outta your mind.

CANDY I'll call.

DAVID Candy, this is Bernie you're talking about.

CANDY Exactly.

DAVID What do you think he did?

CANDY I don't know. But he sure shows up here bloody a lot.

DAVID He does not.

CANDY Didn't they find another girl Saturday morning?

DAVID So?

CANDY What about last week?

DAVID He was in a fight.

CANDY Don't you ever get tired of that story?

DAVID Bernie wouldn't lie to me, Candy.

CANDY Bullshit. I'll call.

CANDY picks up the phone. DAVID grabs it away from her.

DAVID No. I'll call. You're going to feel so stupid.

DAVID dials the phone.

ROBERT, BERNIE and JERRI alone.

ROBERT Fucking women! They're so hard to deal with.

BERNIE Fucking fags!

ROBERT Not like men. A man pisses you off and you can smack him.

JERRI Fucking men!

ROBERT That doesn't work with women. They just get worse if you hit them.

The apartment.

DAVID I see. Thank you very much.

DAVID hangs up the phone. Pause. DAVID does not look at CANDY.

CANDY Well?

DAVID Well—yes there was a fight Friday night. Yes a knife was pulled, yes someone got cut, and yes the cops were called.

CANDY He was probably the one with the knife.

DAVID Stop it.

CANDY What if it was him though. What if he was hurting people and we didn't do anything?

DAVID It's your friends that do the lying.

CANDY Thank you.

DAVID I think you're jealous of Bernie, Candy. I really do.

CANDY Think whatever you like.

CANDY exits. DAVID grabs his cell and dials quickly.

DAVID I need to talk to you. Now.

DAVID hangs up the phone and starts to tear the T-shirt into strips. There is a knock at the door. DAVID guiltily shoves the T-shirt under the futon. Another knock.

Yes?

KANE It's me.

KANE enters.

DAVID Yeah?

KANE It's eight.

DAVID So?

KANE I was supposed to pick you up at eight. Remember?

DAVID Shit—look—something's come up.

KANE David, I've been planning this for a week. I've got the place to myself and everything.

DAVID I can't—

KANE You cancel this and I'll kill you, David.

DAVID All right then.

DAVID takes the T-shirt from under the futon and balls it into his fist.

KANE What's that?

DAVID Something I have to throw in the incinerator on the way out.

DAVID and KANE exit the apartment. BERNIE, alone, laughs quietly.

CANDY enters the apartment.

CANDY David?

There is a knock at the door.

Yes?

ROBERT It's me.

ROBERT enters.

Hi.

Pause.

Can we talk?

CANDY What do you think I am? Some stupid, fat cow you can slap around like a piece of meat? Some bimbo broad who's so desperate for a little affection that she'll put up with anything? You fucking hit me. No one gets away with that!

Pause.

ROBERT I just came to say goodbye. I'm going back to Evelyn.

Pause.

CANDY Goodbye.

ROBERT I'm sorry.

CANDY Fuck you.

ROBERT exits.

KANE's house. DAVID and KANE enter with beers.

KANE You okay?

DAVID Fine.

KANE Something's different tonight.

DAVID I'm wearing underwear. This is quite a place.

KANE Big huh?

DAVID That a real Warhol in the entranceway?

KANE Oh yeah. Dad's into art.

DAVID So what's the big surprise?

KANE Sit down. I'll show you.

DAVID sits. KANE sits next to him and picks up the remote for the DVD player. He turns on the TV. A cheezy TV show theme song begins to play.

CANDY alone.

CANDY Goodbye.

DAVID Oh no!

KANE There you are, David McMillan as Toby.

DAVID Turn it off!

KANE No!

DAVID pulls the remote from KANE's hand and punches off the DVD player and TV.

DAVID What the hell are you doing?

KANE It took me forever to find the DVD.

DAVID That's not me, Kane.

KANE I thought you'd like it.

DAVID You're damaged.

KANE I am not!

DAVID What do you want from me?

KANE I want to be your friend.

DAVID I don't need another friend.

KANE What do you need then?

DAVID I need a lover!

Pause.

KANE I don't think I'm like that.

DAVID Like what?

KANE Queer.

Pause. DAVID moves toward KANE.

DAVID No?

KANE N-no.

DAVID You're scared of me.

KANE *(scared)* I'm not.

DAVID You're scared of what you're feeling.

KANE No.

DAVID takes KANE's head in his hands and holds it very tight. KANE cannot look away.

DAVID I could do anything I want to you and there's not a goddamn thing you could do to stop me. You realize that?

KANE Yes.

DAVID Kiss me.

DAVID lets KANE go. After a brief hesitation KANE kisses DAVID on the lips. Pause.

Now pull your pants down and face the wall.

KANE David, please—

DAVID Do it.

KANE turns his back to DAVID, undoes his pants, and lets them fall. Long pause.

Excited?

KANE Yes.

DAVID Thinking about me?

KANE Yes.

Pause. DAVID moves away from KANE.

DAVID No. You're not like that.

DAVID exits quickly. After a moment KANE pulls up his pants and turns.

KANE David?

The apartment. CANDY enters carrying a bag filled with junk food. She dumps the contents of the bag onto the floor and begins to eat anything she can tear open. This is not a pretty sight.

BENITA's place. DAVID is there.

DAVID I need you to read someone for me.

BENITA Anything for you.

DAVID It might be dangerous.

BENITA To me?

DAVID No.

BERNIE alone.

BERNIE Out of my mind with the smell of blood and cunt
I drive and drive and drive and drive.

BENITA alone. Sings. Overlapping BERNIE.

BENITA Lavender blue dilly dilly
Lavender green…

CANDY alone.

CANDY Stupid pig. Fat cow. Dumb bitch. Fat cow!

JERRI alone.

JERRI I hate her. I hate her. I hate her.

ROBERT alone.

ROBERT Asshole. You stupid fucking asshole. You're such an asshole!

KANE alone.

KANE Everything's fine until you're eleven or twelve—then bang—you've got pubic hair and the party's over.

BENITA The night.

The bar. BERNIE is there. DAVID enters.

DAVID Hey bro!

BERNIE Hey bro!

DAVID Been looking for you all night.

BERNIE Here I am.

DAVID Wanna get crazy?

BERNIE Always.

DAVID I know this girl.

BERNIE You know a girl?

DAVID She'll do us both.

BERNIE About time.

DAVID Yeah.

The apartment. CANDY is eating and crying. Her face is smeared with food. There is a knock at the door. CANDY ignores it. After a moment JERRI enters.

JERRI You really shouldn't leave your door unlocked like that.

CANDY Fuck off!

JERRI Jesus, girl—

CANDY throws a handful of food at JERRI.

CANDY I said fuck off.

JERRI Candy.

CANDY rushes at JERRI and tries to push her out the door.

CANDY Get out! Get out of my house!

JERRI Cut it out.

CANDY Get the fuck out of my house you fat pig!

JERRI pushes CANDY down.

Fuck you!

JERRI No! Fuck you!

DAVID and BERNIE.

DAVID Remember that girl, Cindy?

BERNIE The one with *War and Peace* on her back in braille?

DAVID Yeah.

BERNIE Sure. You fucked her one weekend and I fucked her the next one.

DAVID I never fucked her.

BERNIE No?

DAVID I just said that because I wanted you to think I did.

BERNIE Everyone lies, David.

DAVID Yeah?

BERNIE Yeah.

CANDY and JERRI in the apartment.

JERRI You use people.

CANDY And you don't?

JERRI I was honest with you.

CANDY So was I.

JERRI Like hell! Little Miss Gay-People-Don't-Bother-Me. I guess they only bother you when they want a little more than a few martinis and a quick fuck!

CANDY Dyke!

CANDY slaps JERRI across the face. Pause.

JERRI I should kill you for that.

CANDY Jerri. I'm sorry—I'm—

JERRI Sick. You're sick.

CANDY I didn't mean it!

CANDY puts her arms around JERRI and holds her tight.

JERRI Sick.

CANDY Sorry.

JERRI Let me go.

CANDY I'm so sorry.

BENITA's place. DAVID and BERNIE are there.

BENITA Looking for a little excitement?

DAVID You got it.

BENITA How 'bout you Bernie? Looking for a little excitement?

BERNIE How old are you?

BENITA Everyone asks me that. You're a pretty big guy. I wouldn't stand a chance against either of you. You could do anything you wanted to me.

BERNIE Damn right.

BENITA Like that idea? Mebbe you touch each other accidentally. Feel yourselves in me at the same time.

BERNIE We're not faggots, you know.

DAVID I am.

BERNIE We're just a coupla buddies out for a good time. Don't try to make it dirty.

BENITA You're awful touchy, Bernie.

BERNIE Why don't you take your top off?

BENITA I think you'd rather do it for me.

BERNIE Fuckin' rights.

BERNIE tears off BENITA's top.

You got no fuckin' tits.

BENITA You have trouble makin' it with people with no tits, Bernie?

DAVID I prefer it.

BENITA Bet you like big, fat, squishy watermelon tits.

BERNIE Lay down.

BENITA Not yet.

BERNIE roughly pushes her to the bed.

BERNIE I said lay down.

DAVID Bernie!

BENITA It's okay, Davey. Bernie likes to play rough.

BERNIE His name's David.

BENITA Mebbe I should just call him sir.

BERNIE Take your skirt off.

BENITA Make me.

BERNIE pulls off her skirt.

Ooh.

BERNIE And the nylons.

BENITA What's the point?

BERNIE Do it.

BENITA removes her nylons. BERNIE grabs them and hands them to DAVID.

Tie her up.

DAVID Uh—Bernie—

BERNIE Do it.

DAVID ties BENITA's hands.

DAVID I'm not hurting you, am I?

BERNIE Who cares?

BENITA It's all right, Davey.

BERNIE slaps BENITA.

BERNIE It's David.

DAVID Bernie!

BERNIE His name's David.

BENITA Davey.

He slaps BENITA again.

BERNIE David.

BENITA Okay. David! David!

DAVID Look—maybe this wasn't such a great idea.

BERNIE It's a terrific idea.

DAVID It's getting too weird. I don't—

BERNIE Don't be such a pussy. She's no one.

DAVID No. Bernie—

BERNIE moves behind DAVID and puts his arms around him. He pushes his body up tight against DAVID's back and strokes DAVID's body.

BERNIE You'll like it.

KANE alone.

KANE I'll fall.

BERNIE Trust me.

DAVID No. We can't—

BERNIE Relax bro. It's just you and me.

DAVID She's my friend.

BERNIE I'm your friend. I'm your best friend.

BERNIE has worked his hands inside DAVID's pants. He strokes DAVID's cock.

DAVID Jesus.

BERNIE Us.

DAVID Don't.

DAVID and BERNIE kiss ferociously. BENITA leads them to the bed. Lights rise on the apartment. CANDY is cleaning up her mess.

JERRI Look at me.

CANDY I'm so ashamed.

Pause.

JERRI It's not me, is it?

CANDY shakes her head.

I thought it was something I was doing. Is there anyone you can love?

CANDY David. Maybe.

Pause.

It's me.

JERRI Candy, I'm sorry.

JERRI starts to exit.

CANDY Jerri?

JERRI What?

CANDY Do you think I'm fat?

JERRI goes to CANDY and puts her arms around her.

JERRI I think you're the most beautiful woman I've ever seen. I always have.

JERRI kisses CANDY on the forehead then exits.

BENITA's place. DAVID and BERNIE are sleeping in the bed. BENITA is watching them from a chair. BERNIE wakes, sits up and looks at her.

BERNIE I'm his friend.

BENITA You were.

BERNIE What did you do to me? When you thought I was sleeping?

BENITA Touched your head.

BERNIE I felt something. Inside me. It kinda hurt.

BENITA Now you know what it's like.

BERNIE He needs me.

BENITA He's learning.

BERNIE He couldn't live without me.

BENITA Why couldn't you get your cock hard?

BERNIE I'm his best friend.

BERNIE moves to BENITA quickly and puts his hands around her throat.

BENITA What about David?

BERNIE I can handle David.

BENITA Sure about that?

Pause. BERNIE removes his hands from BENITA's throat.

BENITA moves away from him. BERNIE looks at DAVID.

BERNIE He looks like a kid.

BENITA He's not.

BERNIE What did you see? Inside my head?

BENITA Fear.

BERNIE You're all the same—you know that? You're jealous of us.

BENITA We handle it.

BERNIE Aren't you scared of me?

BENITA There are scarier monsters.

BERNIE I like you. You're bright.

BENITA Go away.

Pause.

BERNIE If you tell him it'll only screw him up more.

BENITA He knows!

Long pause.

BERNIE He told you?

BENITA Goodbye, Bernie.

BERNIE He told you?

BENITA Get out.

BERNIE looks at DAVID for a long moment, then exits.

Davey, it's time to wake up.

The apartment. CANDY is alone. There is a knock at the door. CANDY goes to it.

CANDY Yes?

KANE enters.

KANE Is David in?

CANDY No.

KANE Do you know when he'll be back?

CANDY No. I'll tell him you came by.

KANE No. Don't. I'll drop by later. I'd like to surprise him.

CANDY All right.

KANE exits.

BENITA's place. DAVID is still sleeping.

BENITA Davey?

DAVID Bernie?

BENITA Gone.

DAVID dresses.

DAVID I passed right out. You okay?

BENITA He's doing it.

DAVID No.

BENITA Yes.

DAVID He's my friend. He'd never—

BENITA Stop him.

DAVID I can't.

BENITA You have to.

Pause.

DAVID Yes.

The apartment. CANDY is alone.

CANDY I hate my job. I hate my life. I hate this city. I hate myself. Jesus. I hate myself.

DAVID enters.

DAVID I lied. There was no fight at the Crest.

KANE alone.

KANE I lied.

CANDY David—no.

DAVID He's doing it.

CANDY Call the police.

DAVID I've got to find him.

CANDY I'll come.

DAVID No.

CANDY Be careful.

DAVID I always am. Lock the door.

DAVID exits. CANDY goes to the phone and dials. BERNIE is heard singing, very quietly, from somewhere nearby. CANDY straightens nervously and stops dialing. BERNIE enters singing and stares at CANDY. CANDY carefully hangs up the phone.

CANDY Bernie…

BERNIE How ya doin'?

CANDY How did you get in?

BERNIE David's window. Thought I'd wait in the bedroom.

CANDY You should go, Bernie.

BERNIE Boy, that David's got some crazy ideas huh?

CANDY He just wants to talk to you.

BERNIE Why do you hate me?

CANDY I don't.

BERNIE It's because of Dana, isn't it?

CANDY That was a long time ago.

BERNIE Do you think I'm the only one who let her down?

CANDY Shut up, Bernie.

BERNIE She was stupid.

CANDY No—

BERNIE She deserved to die. I was glad she died. I should've killed her. I wish I had.

BERNIE advances on CANDY.

CANDY Bernie—please—

BERNIE I'm not gonna hurt you.

CANDY Good.

BERNIE It's just that—me and David—we're goin' away. Together. Away.

CANDY Great.

BERNIE He wanted me to clean up.

BERNIE grabs CANDY by the throat.

CANDY Don't!

There is a knock at the door. CANDY and BERNIE freeze.

Let me go.

After a moment BERNIE relaxes his grip on CANDY's neck. She moves away from him. KANE enters. CANDY grabs him.

Kane! Come in!

KANE Thanks. Hi Bernie.

BERNIE Hello.

CANDY Bernie was just leaving.

KANE Yeah?

CANDY David's looking for Bernie. A lot of people are looking for Bernie.

KANE Oh?

BERNIE Yes.

CANDY Goodbye Bernie.

BERNIE exits.

KANE Booga booga. What's wrong with him?

CANDY Call the police, Kane.

KANE Why?

CANDY Just do it, Kane!

BERNIE's place. DAVID enters carrying a twenty-two. He sits in a chair with the rifle across his lap. He sings softly to himself. All characters are in isolation.

JERRI Her hair.

ROBERT Her skin.

KANE David.

CANDY David.

BERNIE Candy.

DAVID Bernie.

BERNIE enters his house.

BERNIE Candy said you'd be here.

DAVID You better not have hurt her.

BERNIE She's fine. How'd you get in?

DAVID Basement window.

BERNIE We're good at that.

DAVID I found Linda in the freezer.

BERNIE Ah. *(short pause)* You never liked her.

DAVID I thought I knew you.

BERNIE You do, David. You're just like me.

DAVID No.

BERNIE Yes.

DAVID Shut up!

BERNIE You're awful upset, pal.

DAVID You asshole.

BERNIE David, calm down.

BERNIE reaches into his pocket and drops a number of mismatched earrings as he speaks.

They weren't anyone that mattered. They were secretaries, waitresses, nurses—hairdressers, for Christ's sake.

DAVID Jesus.

BERNIE They weren't important.

DAVID Yes they were.

BERNIE To who?

DAVID To their families. Themselves. To me.

BERNIE You? Get real, David. No one's ever mattered to you in your life.

DAVID That's not true.

BERNIE You don't give a shit about people. They drop in and out of your life all the time. Who cares how they feel? There's only been one person you ever really cared about. Me.

DAVID You're sick.

BERNIE Sick? Sick like getting your cock sucked in a car by guys you don't even know. Fucking someone in the dark that you can't even see. Playing head games with some stupid boy.

DAVID Shut up, Bernie!

BERNIE Too close for comfort, pal?

DAVID I mean it.

BERNIE Let's drop the shit for once. We're the ones with the brains, David. We're the ones with the power.

DAVID What power?

BERNIE The power to make people do whatever we want to.

KANE speaks from the darkness.

KANE I don't think I'm like that.

DAVID raises the gun and points it at BERNIE's face.

DAVID I don't know you anymore.

BERNIE Remember when my dad gave me that rifle?

DAVID Stop it.

BERNIE Just before that camping trip when you told me you loved me. We shot that one partridge. Remember how good you felt when you shot it? You said you'd never killed anything before. You said it was a rush. That was how I felt when Dana killed herself.

DAVID I'm going to stop you, Bernie.

BERNIE Yeah?

BERNIE moves forward and takes the end of the gun in his mouth. He and DAVID stare at one another. DAVID removes the gun from BERNIE's mouth and begins to exit. BERNIE grabs him desperately.

Stay with me, David. We'll go away. Somewhere where they don't know me. I won't do it again.

DAVID It's too late.

BERNIE No one has to know. Nothing has to change.

DAVID Bernie, Candy knows. Benita knows.

BERNIE It's your fault! It's because you left! I could control it when you were around!

DAVID Don't, Bernie.

BERNIE I'll keep doing it, David. I will.

DAVID tries to pull away from BERNIE. BERNIE holds him tighter.

You'll have no friends! You'll be alone!

DAVID Let me go, Bernie!

BERNIE They'll hurt me, David. They'll put me in jail—they'll—

BERNIE is cut off by the sound of a distant siren.

Don't leave me again.

DAVID I'm sorry.

BERNIE Please.

DAVID picks up the rifle and holds it out to BERNIE.

I thought you loved me.

DAVID places the rifle in BERNIE's hands.

DAVID I do.

DAVID exits. The lights begin to fade on BERNIE as the sound of the siren rises. BENITA sings as the lights rise on all the other characters alone, except for BERNIE.

BENITA Lavender blue dilly dilly
Lavender green
When I am king dilly dilly
You shall be queen…

There is the loud explosion of a gunshot. Lights on all other characters snap to black. There is a beat of silence then a phone begins to ring. Lights rise on the apartment. DAVID is sitting on the futon. CANDY enters with a pizza and a six-pack of Coke. She juggles the food as she answers the phone.

CANDY Hello. Just a sec. David, it's Sal for you.

Pause. He doesn't look at her.

David. Sal's on the phone.

Pause.

Sal, look—he's still not up for calls. Do me a favour and try again tomorrow. Thanks. You're a doll.

CANDY hangs up the phone and opens the pizza and a Coke.

Rose Bowl special. Anchovies, pepperoni and green peppers.

She eats some pizza as she looks at DAVID.

How long do I have to put up with this?

Pause.

It wasn't your fault.

Pause.

Bernie was sick.

Pause.

None of us realized how sick he was.

Pause.

You can't let him ruin your life, David. He's done that to too many other people already.

Pause.

You've got to get out of here. Go see Rod—or Sal.

DAVID I can't.

There is a knock at the door.

I'm not home.

CANDY Yes?

KANE enters.

Hiya, guy.

KANE How is he?

CANDY Fucked.

KANE Hi David.

DAVID I'm not home.

Pause. KANE starts to exit. CANDY turns him back to DAVID.

CANDY Talk to him.

CANDY exits.

KANE So—uh—how's it going?

Pause.

Everyone's asking about you at work. Regulars are still requesting your section. They hired a new bus boy. They—uh—they want to make me a waiter, David.

DAVID You?

KANE Can you believe it?

DAVID No.

Pause.

KANE I'm sorry about Bernie—and everything else.

Pause.

You—uh—you mind if I have a slice of pizza? I'm starving.

KANE helps himself to a piece of pizza.

That's great. Rose Bowl?

Pause. KANE kisses DAVID on the lips tenderly. Pause.

Say something.

DAVID You got pizza on the futon.

KANE What?

DAVID There!

KANE Shit! I'm sorry.

DAVID Candy, Kane got pizza on the futon!

CANDY enters.

CANDY What?

KANE It was an accident. I'm sorry.

CANDY Don't worry about it.

Pause.

DAVID It's fucked.

CANDY You okay?

DAVID Nope.

KANE Anything I can do?

DAVID Nope.

Pause.

I get so scared sometimes.

CANDY Join the club.

KANE I'm always scared.

DAVID I've never told either of you—

CANDY Puh-lease.

KANE It's okay.

CANDY We know.

DAVID Yeah?

CANDY Yeah.

BENITA alone.

BENITA I love you.

Slow fade to black.

photo by David Hawe

Brad Fraser is one of Canada's best known playwrights, in addition to being a director for stage and film, a talk show host and many other things. Born in Edmonton, Alberta in 1959, he won his first playwriting competition at the age of seventeen and has been writing ever since.

His plays include: *Unidentified Human Remains and the True Nature of Love; Poor Super Man* (both named as one of the year's ten best by *Time* Magazine); *Martin Yesterday; Outrageous; Snake in Fridge* and *Cold Meat Party*, (both commissioned by the Royal Exchange Theatre in Manchester, England); *Mutants; Wolfboy; Rude Noises; Chainsaw Love, Young Art; Return of the Bride; The Ugly Man*; and *Prom Night of the Living Dead*.

Brad's plays have won numerous awards, including *The London Evening Standard* Award for Most Promising Playwright, The L.A. Critics Award, The Dora Mavor Moore Award, and London's *Time Out* Award for Best New Play. Brad is a five-time winner of the Alberta Culture Playwrighting Competition and a two-time winner of the prestigious Chalmers Award.

In addition to his work as a playwright and director, Brad writes for print media, radio, film and television, including the movie "Leaving Metropolis," which he also directed. (Winner of the Sydney Gay and Lesbian Film Festival Audience favourite award and currently available on DVD in Canada and America).

Visit Brad's website at www.Bradfraser.net.